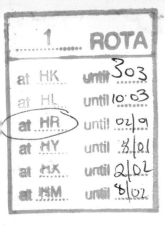

The Illustrated Guide to

WITCHCRAFT

The Secrets of Wicca and Paganism Revealed

TONY AND AILEEN GRIST

The Illustrated Guide to

WITCHCRAFT

The Secrets of Wicca and Paganism Revealed

TONY AND AILEEN GRIST

A GODSFIELD BOOK

First published in Great Britain in 2000
by Godsfield Press Ltd
A division of David and Charles Ltd
Laurel House, Station Approach,
New Alresford, Hants SO24 9JH, UK

10 9 8 7 6 5 4 3 2 1

© 2000 Godsfield Press
Text © 2000 Tony and Aileen Grist

Designed for Godsfield Press by
The Bridgewater Book Company
Photographer *Ian Parsons*
Illustrator *Sharon Harmer*
Picture researcher *Liz Eddison*

Printed and bound in Hong Kong

ISBN 1–84181–003–7

Acknowledgements
The publishers would like to thank the following for the use of pictures:

AKG Photo: pp 17, 18, 20, 21, 22, 33, 35, 38, 45, 70
The Bridgeman Art Library: pp 19, 20, 21, 34, 48, 63, 102
e.t.archive: pp 52, 53, 66, 80, 82
Fortean Picture Library: pp 9, 10, 11, 30, 31
The Garden Picture Library: p 49
Hulton Getty Images: pp 9, 15
The Image Bank: pp 31, 34, 49, 111
Tony Stone Images: pp 12, 17, 34

Special thanks to
F Annette, G Applebee, J Bichard, A Bill, H Burchell, RJ Clarke, A Ferguson,
D Goddard, C Hasler, L Hill, P James, L Lassalle, J Manze, R Nobbs, C Oxley,
C Southern, J Thursfield, Trisha, R Wilding for help with photography

Special thanks for help with properties to

Curiouser and Curiouser (jewelry) and Hocus Pocus in Brighton, UK, and especially to

Ralph Harvey, The Order of Artemis Wiccan Traditionalists, Hove, UK

CONTENTS

1 | Who, What, When, and Why?

Wicca is a very old religion and yet also a very new one. It draws upon the distant past to forge a spirituality that addresses the issues of the modern age. Wiccans worship goddess and god as equal and complementary partners in the ongoing work of creation. Like all living religions, Wicca is in a continual process of change and development.

Wicca is also a craft. It is something you believe in but also something that you do. Wiccans are practical people who seek to better themselves and the world through ritual and the judicious use of magic.

What you have in your hands is a Book of Shadows. *The first written "Book of Shadows" was compiled by Gerald Gardner. Traditionally, the Book of Shadows is passed on from coven leader to initiate, to be copied out in a black book in their own "hand of write"—their own handwriting. The original Gardnerian* Book of Shadows *(see page 10), assembled in the 1950s, was a scrapbook of instructions and rituals. No standard copy of it exists; handwritten copies of the book have been changed, adapted, and personalized as they have been handed down via initiates. The* Book of Shadows *is in fact an open-ended working document. Most Wiccans either use the Gardnerian book as a foundation to which their own material is added, or else construct their own book from scratch.*

This book contains everything you need to set out on the Wiccan path—think of it as a basic tool kit. While the basic philosophy of this book is Gardnerian, most of the material is new.

Wicca is a serious business, but not a solemn one. Your gods and goddesses will become your closest friends, and you will want to treat them as such—with respect, love, and humor.

The History of Wicca

Wicca is also known as Witchcraft, The Craft, Craft of the Wise, and Wise Craft. Its true history is shrouded in mystery, although there have always been people who were said to be witches. Only in the twentieth century, with the repeal of the Witchcraft Act in the United Kingdom in the early 1950s, did Wicca emerge as a living religion. It has since spread throughout the world.

WITCH HUNTING

Stories about witches can be found in the Bible (Exodus 22:18; 2 Chronicles 33:6) and in Roman texts such as Apuleius's *Golden Ass.* Over the centuries throughout Europe and North America, thousands of men, women, and children have been tortured, tried, and executed (or lynched) for the crime of practicing "witchcraft." The most famous witchcraft persecutions occurred in the seventeenth century. Up until 1951, when the British Witchcraft Act was repealed, people could still be tried and imprisoned in the UK; the last such case involved spirit medium Helen Duncan, who was sent to jail during the Second World War.

But all of this is merely evidence for a belief in witches, not for their actual existence. Arthur Miller's play *The Crucible*, about the witch hunt in Salem, Massachusetts, demonstrates how easily a community can be swept along in the hysteria of witch hunting. People can be made to confess to anything under torture and psychological pressure. Many of those who were being tortured under suspicion of practicing witchcraft simply told the inquisitors what they wanted to hear. Others may have been self-deluding fantasists. We cannot say that all of the material that came out of the witchcraft trials is untrue, but neither can we put much trust in it.

WISE WOMAN AND CUNNING MAN

Fact or fiction, the image of the cauldron-stirring, broomstick-riding witch is part of the inheritance of modern Wicca. For the inquisitors it was an image of female depravity; for the modern Wiccan it has become an image of feminine strength and independence. Equally important for the modern Wiccan is the image of the village wise woman or cunning man: herbalist, healer, and expert in simple spellcraft. Such people certainly existed—and still do exist—though whether they would have thought of themselves as witches (let alone Wiccans) is highly debatable.

A REBIRTH OF PAGANISM

What can be said with confidence is that magic and paganism were in the air in Britain in the first half of the twentieth century. The Magical Order of the Golden

ABOVE: *In this traditional image of witchcraft, three naked witches create a magical brew while a fourth rides to a sabbat on a goat.*

Dawn, founded at the end of the nineteenth century, provided the impetus for a great occult revival and helped launch the careers of the famous magicians Aleister Crowley and Dion Fortune. Pagan themes are explicit in the work of popular writers such as Kenneth Grahame and Rudyard Kipling. The scholarly investigation of myth and folk tradition produced highly influential books, such as Sir James Frazer's *The Golden Bough,* Margaret Murray's *The Witch Cult in Western Europe,* and *The White Goddess* by Robert Graves.

THE WITCHES OF CHESHIRE

Many modern Wiccans claim to belong to local traditions that go back many decades. Bob Clay-Egerton, a much-loved and admired British Wiccan occultist, who died in 1998, gave circumstantial accounts of the activities of a coven that used the caverns and

ABOVE: *Alderley Edge in Cheshire is a meeting place of British witches. The hillside is honeycombed with caves and disused mine workings. Bob Clay-Egerton and Alex Sanders both worked here.*

LEFT: *Aleister Crowley (1875–1947) was the most famous magician of the 20th century. His work influenced Gerald Gardner—Gardner may have paid Crowley to write rituals for him.*

mineshafts around Alderley Edge in Cheshire in the United Kingdom in the 1940s. Clay-Egerton claimed to have been initiated into this coven himself and told anecdotally how walkers on the Edge were sometimes disturbed to hear ghostly music floating up from inside the earth. This was not due to boggarts (goblins), but to local witches, who were playing gramophone records during their underground rituals. He believed that this coven had been in existence since the mid-nineteenth century. Unfortunately, although his stories seem plausible, they cannot be proven.

GERALD GARDNER

Wicca emerged into the light in about 1950 with the publication of two books by retired colonial civil servant Gerald Gardner—*Witchcraft Today* and *The Meaning of Witchcraft*. Gardner was born in 1884, and worked most notably as a civil servant for the colonial government in Malaya and Borneo. He was also an active Freemason.

Gardner maintained that he had been initiated into a witch cult whose origins went back into prehistory—the New Forest Coven—in the late 1930s. He was influenced by the scholar and archaeologist Margaret Murray, who had argued in a succession of very popular books, including *The Witch Cult in Western Europe* and *The God of the Witches*, that medieval witchcraft was nothing other than the old pagan religion of Britain gone underground. These days most historians tend to dismiss Margaret Murray's theories as wishful thinking.

ABOVE: *Gerald Gardner (1884–1964) created the modern Wiccan movement. His teachings and rituals, known as* The Book of Shadows, *form the basis of all later developments.*

SECRET TRADITION

It is still disputed whether Gardner founded Wicca or simply publicized an existing tradition. His Wicca was supposed to be a secret tradition, but its rituals soon found their way into print. Gardner published some himself, and his disciples followed his lead and published more. Some of the materials in the so-called *Book of Shadows* may be traditional and ancient. Some, we know, were

ABOVE: *Freemasonry is a secret society. It expresses spiritual truths using symbols from the builders' craft. Gardner was a mason and drew on Masonic models to create his own rituals.*

written by Gardner himself and one of his high priestesses, Doreen Valiente. Others were borrowed from writers as diverse as Crowley and Kipling. There is a persistent rumor that Gardner paid Crowley to write rituals for him. Valiente is on record as saying she disliked the Crowleyian tone of some of Gardner's early rituals and rewrote them accordingly. All the Gardnerian material has been published in Janet and Stewart Farrar's *Eight Sabbats for Witches* and *The Witches' Way*.

ALEX SANDERS

Gardner was a charismatic and mischievous character. He enjoyed the notoriety that his witchcraft revival brought him and was happy to ham it up for the benefit of the press. After Gardner's death in 1964, his mantle passed to a young man called Alex Sanders. Sanders claimed to represent an entirely independent tradition called Alexandrian Wicca, when he was merely giving a personal twist to the Gardnerian material. For years the two traditions existed in mutual antipathy. In fact, there was little difference between them. Sanders had a background in ceremonial magic, so his form of Wicca has a more formal character, while the Gardnerian version of Wicca is folksier. These days it is unlikely that anyone still practices a "pure" version of either. Their rituals are fairly interchangeable.

LEFT: *Starhawk (pen name of Miriam Simos) is a leading American Wiccan. In her teaching Wicca acquires a politically radical and feminist edge. Her best known book is* The Spiral Dance.

Sanders liked to shock. He once said that if the Roman Catholic church continued to badmouth him he would use his magical powers to wipe it out. Gardnerian Wicca was a little stuffy and prissy and more than a little exclusive. Sanders democratized it.

DIVERSIFICATION

After Sanders, Wicca set off in so many different directions at once that its history becomes all but impossible to chart. Today there are almost as many different traditions operating as there are high priests and high priestesses.

No two practitioners work in exactly the same way or hold exactly the same beliefs:

• English Wiccan Vivianne Crowley (no relation to Aleister Crowley) interprets Wicca in the light of Jungian psychology.

• American witch Starhawk works to a radical political and feminist agenda.

On the one hand there is the high priestess who insists on her initiates being able to identify individual types of trees, on the other hand there is the one who says that her idea of a nature ritual is to throw open the window—where others hug trees she hugs lampposts!

The most important point to bear in mind when practicing your own version of Wicca is that there are no absolute rights and wrongs. Wicca is the do-it-yourself religion.

Wiccan Beliefs

Wicca is a religion without a creed. There is no Wiccan Holy Book. Wicca is not a system of beliefs but a system of values. It is a religion rooted in the rhythms and cycles of nature, and its values arise from the observation and celebration of the natural world. These values include a respect for life, a cheerful acceptance of the facts of life—including sex and death—and a feeling for the magical and numinous. Wiccans are, or should be, realists. Their religion is based on experience —not on theological speculation.

LIVING EARTH

Most Wiccans believe that the Earth is a living being whom we need to honor. She is our Mother and we are Her children. Wiccans try to minimize the damage they do to Her in their daily lives. Many Wiccans are active in the ecological movement. Wiccans see themselves not as separate from nature, but as part of it, with responsibilities to protect and guard the less conscious life around them.

BELOW: *The Earth is our Mother and we are Her children. Wiccans try to minimize the damage they do to nature in their daily lives.*

GODDESS AND GOD

Most Wiccans believe that the divine is both male and female. For some this means acknowledging a single goddess and a single god. For others it means worshiping any number of gods and goddesses selected from the pagan pantheons—that is, any of the Greek, Celtic, Roman, Aztec etc. gods or goddesses. The Goddess of the Witches is frequently invoked as a trinity of Maiden, Mother, and Crone. The God of the Witches is most commonly represented as a man with horns or antlers, or as the "Green Man" (made up of living greenery), a character often written about, notably by Kathleen Basford and Ronald Miller, both in books entitled *The Green Man*.

LEFT: *The Christian Devil, here shown as he appears in the tarot, is a perversion of the Wiccan Horned God. Horns were a common attribute of gods in ancient cultures.*

LEFT: *The Wiccan God is commonly represented as the Green Man—a spirit of the wild woods, made up of greenery or sprouting it from mouth and nostrils.*

Wicca takes its god forms from the religions of antiquity and is independent of Christianity. The horned god of Wicca is not the Christian devil: the Christian devil is a demonization of pagan god forms. Horns used to be a common attribute of gods in ancient cultures. They are considered to be a symbol of male authority and sexual potency. Goddesses can wear horns too—Hathor, the Egyptian Goddess of Love, for example.

Belief in a god and goddess does not necessarily imply literal belief. On the one hand, some Wiccans are happy to see their gods and goddesses as real beings "out there"; on the other hand, however, others view them as personifications of natural forces or as purely imaginary characters whose myths help us make sense of human experience.

Most Wiccans worry very little about the exact status of their belief because they are pragmatists. If a goddess works for you, why bother with the unanswerable questions about who or what she is?

FREEDOM FROM DOCTRINE

This pragmatism extends across the board. Wiccans believe in magic because they do spells and healing and get results.

They believe in spirits because they encounter them. They believe in reincarnation when they have memories of previous lives.

None of these beliefs has any doctrinal force, and it is quite possible to be a Wiccan and a total skeptic at the same time.

It is also possible to be a Wiccan and a Christian who goes to church regularly (though some priests might be unhappy if they found out) or an observant Jew (or a member of any other religious group).

The important point to remember is that it is not belief that makes you a Wiccan, but what you do and what you are.

Wiccan Ethics

Wiccan ethics are summed up in "The Wiccan Rede" (also known as the Wiccan law), "An it harm none, do what you will." This is close to St. Augustine's summary of Christian ethics, "Love, and do what you will." Wiccans believe in balancing personal freedom with respect for the freedom of others. They talk seriously of a Law of Threefold Return—whatever you do you get back three times over. Curse and you will be cursed; bless and you will be blessed.

KARMA

"Black magic" is casting spells to harm others. No reputable Wiccan will have anything to do with black magic. Rogue practitioners may call themselves witches but they are not accepted by the Wiccan community. Casting spells to help others without their consent is "gray magic" at best. Wiccans avoid this, too. We have no right to manipulate others without them knowing, even if it seems to be for their own good.

Every act has consequences for the person who does it. Think of an ax used to chop down a tree. At first it appears that only the tree suffers; what can a tree do to an ax? However, the ax is blunted by the act of chopping and, if left in contact, the sap from the tree will cause the ax to rust if it is not cleaned properly. Whatever you do will, sometimes very subtly, affect you. It may be that the person you injure will retaliate; it may simply be that your conscience will make you suffer. More profoundly, the doing of evil coarsens and corrupts the soul. The principle at work here is that which Hindus call the Law of Karma. It is expressed in the Bible by the proverb: "You reap what you sow."

Of course, this cosmic principle applies to good acts as well. Bless others and you will receive threefold blessings in return.

ABOVE: *Every act has consequences for the doer. An ax looks invulnerable but is blunted by the tree it chops down and corroded by its sap.*

RIGHT: *Candles, dolls (also known as* poppets *and* fif-fafs)*, amulets, talismans, and herbs: these are some of the things that can be used to focus energy when helping others in spellcraft.*

BREAKING THE RULES

There are times when rules have to be broken. Wiccans have been known to do magical work against criminals. For example, one coven performed a binding spell to assist in the capture of a notorious rapist. It worked. And there is the story of the English witches getting together to perform strong magic to keep Hitler from invading the United Kingdom in 1940. But in these cases, as in all others, there is a cost. According to Gardner, the amount of psychic energy expended in the "Battle of Britain" spell was so great that some of the older participants took sick and died.

SEX IN THE COVEN

Wiccans celebrate and enjoy their sexuality – all the more reason for them to have strict rules about the place of sex in coven life. Sex is a powerful force; it can liberate but it can also enslave. It can be loving but also abusive. The coven leader who uses his or her position of power to obtain sexual favors from initiates is acting in defiance of the Wiccan Rede. Responsible covens operate on the understanding that there will be no sexual shenanigans between members and turn away potential recruits who seem to be thrill-seekers.

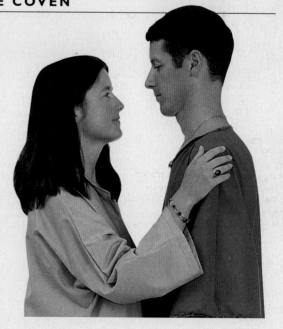

Gods and Goddesses

Gerald Gardner was ahead of his time. Writers such as Robert Graves and Margaret Murray had prepared the ground, but Gardner was the first person to publicly proclaim himself a practicing goddess worshiper, some thirty years before the New Age movement made it fashionable. A devotion to the goddess is the most distinctive and revolutionary thing about Wicca. Wiccans also worship a god, but he is not the omnipotent "father god" of other traditions, but the goddess's equal partner in the work of creation and evolution.

THE DIVINE IN EVERYTHING

Wiccans believe that the goddess and god are active in everything. They are the forces that light the stars and bring the flowers to birth. They are the breath of life. Every being, including every human being, is a miniature of the universe, and the god and goddess forces are active in everyone. The first place to look for the goddess and god is in your heart.

LORD AND LADY

Traditional Wiccans often refer to their god and goddess as the Lord and the Lady. They are not distant beings with no name, but ever present friends and companions.

The Lady is associated with the fertile earth and the moon. As Moon Goddess she has four aspects: waxing, full, waning, and dark. The first three correspond to the three ages of woman—Maiden, Mother, and Crone. The fourth aspect represents the unknowable mystery of death and "unbeing," and the darkness of the womb from which all life comes.

The Lord is associated with the wild places of the earth and the wild beasts. He is

ABOVE: *The Moon Goddess has four aspects: waxing, full, waning, and dark. The first three are represented by Maiden, Mother, and Crone; the last represents the unknowable mystery of unbeing.*

BELOW: *A Wiccan God dies and rises again. He is identified with the rising and setting of the sun, and with the life cycle of vegetation.*

ABOVE: *Wiccans worship God and Goddess as equals, here represented by the interlocked astrological symbols of Mars and Venus.*

sun and rain and all that drives forward the forces of creation. Sometimes he is pictured as the sacrificial king who gives his life for the land. But if he dies he also rises again, as the sun does and as vegetation does after its (apparent) death during the winter months. His death and resurrection encourage human hopes of immortality.

The goddess and god are lovers and partners. Wicca frankly acknowledges sexuality as the motor force of nature—"It's love that makes the world go round."

ABOVE: *Pan is the Greek God of Shepherding and Wild Nature. His innocent sexuality is portrayed in this image of him frolicking with a Nymph, by 19th century artist Arnold Bocklin.*

OLD HORNIE

The Wiccan god is often depicted as having horns. This does not make him the Christian devil. Christian artists originally took the image of Pan, Greek God of Shepherding and Wild Nature, and applied it to the personification of evil.

It is common for incoming religions to demonize the gods they have overthrown. In ancient times horns were simply a symbol of fertility and divine authority. In most cultures they were worn by both goddesses and gods. A misreading of the Old Testament led to Moses being shown with horns in medieval art. He wears them proudly in Michelangelo's famous statue in the church of San Pietro in Vincoli in Rome.

MANY GODS

The Lord and Lady have many names. The Lady is known as Diana, Aradia, Frau Venus, and Holda. The Lord is known as Herne, Cernnunos, and Pan. These names are, however, only the beginning. The realities of the divine are too complex to be contained in a single image or a single identity.

In the mythologies of ancient and traditional cultures we find gods and goddesses of all shapes and sizes. Some are all-powerful and wide-ranging, such as Jupiter; others are local, such as Coventina, who was worshiped at one particular spring on Hadrian's Wall.

There are even comical gods, such as Baubo, who cheered up the mourning Earth Mother Demeter by exposing her own genitals (her genitals looked like a comical face). There are gods and goddesses for almost anything. The ever practical Romans, for example, had a Goddess of Plumbing and Drains called Cloacina.

You could think of the divine as a diamond with many facets. Each of these facets is a god or goddess. Each flashes out a different aspect of the one truth.

IMAGINATION AND EXPLORATION

By exploring the world of the gods and goddesses Wiccans are exploring the hinterland of the human imagination. Jung called it the *collective unconscious*. Occultists refer to it as the *inner planes*. Here we make contact with deep and ancient mysteries, drawing tight the chain that links us to our ancestors.

There are many Pagan pantheons. Some Wiccans draw on a mixture of several pantheons, while others work with only one.

GREECE AND ROME

The most accessible of the pantheons are those of Greece and Rome. This is because the Greeks and Romans had a

BELOW: *Celtic mythology haunts the legends of King Arthur. The Holy Grail was originally a mystical cauldron of plenty. Here it appears to the Round Table in a 15th century French book illustration.*

written culture and their mythologies have come down to us largely intact. All through the Middle Ages Latin was the language of scholarship and diplomacy. By keeping Latin alive the Roman Catholic church kept the old deities alive too. Juno and Jupiter, Mars and Venus all flourish in the poems of Shakespeare and Keats and the paintings of Titian and Poussin. Medieval science used them too—they are forces in alchemy and astrology. Look up at the night sky and there they still are, embodied in planets and constellations.

THE NORTHERN TRADITION

The deities of the Northern tradition— Scandinavian, German, Anglo-Saxon—are also easily accessed. The mythologies of these deities were committed to writing during the Christian era, notably by Snorri Sturluson in the *Prose Edda* (c.1230 C.E.). Although the myths are admittedly warlike, they are free from racism and bigotry, despite the recent notoriety brought about by Wagner's operas.

THE CELTS

The Celtic gods and goddesses of Ireland, Scotland, Wales, and Ancient Britain are hugely popular. Since their stories were passed on verbally, much has been lost. They haunt the *Mabinogion*—four tales in the fourteenth century Welsh text *The Red Book of Hergest*—and the legends of King Arthur and many of the modern fantasy cycles. The

ABOVE: *The Egyptian Goddess Bast was represented as a cat. Cats were sacred to the ancient Egyptians and their mummified remains frequently turn up in archeological digs.*

writers of the Celtic twilight at the end of the nineteenth century— for example, W.B. Yeats and Fiona Macleod—helped to create the romantic ethos out of which modern Wicca was born.

THE EGYPTIANS

Pagan Egypt lives on its monuments. The Western magical traditions exist in its shadow. The Egyptians had deities in the shape of not only humans, but also animals, for example, Bast the Cat Goddess. The glamor of Egyptian archaeology has established this strange world and its gods and goddesses in the modern Western consciousness.

POPULAR CULTURE

The ancient goddesses and gods continue to be a living force in popular culture. They appear in comic books, movies, and television shows such as *Hercules* and *Xena—Warrior Princess*. The world of commerce knows their value—many examples have been used to brand companies and their products. For example, Nike is not only a brand of sportswear but the Greek goddess of Victory. Mercury Telecommunications is named after the Roman Messenger of the Gods.

ABOVE: *Figures from Greek and Roman mythology are immortalized in the heavens. The constellation of the Little Bear represents Arcas, the ill-fated son of Jupiter and the nymph Callisto.*

Who's Who

Most Pagan religions recognize thousands of gods and goddesses. The Romans, for example, had gods and goddesses for every town, river, and hill throughout the Empire. Here are a few preeminent gods and goddesses from a range of traditions. Remember—all the gods are one god and all the goddesses one goddess.

ABOVE: *Horus is an Egyptian Sun God. He is the son of Isis and Osiris, and is represented by a falcon or a man with a falcon's head.*

RIGHT: *Isis, the Egyptian Great Mother Goddess, is here shown suckling the infant Horus. Her headdress combines the sun disk with the cow's horns of Hathor Goddess of Love.*

ANUBIS: Egyptian God of the Underworld; depicted with a jackal's head.

APHRODITE: Greek Goddess of Love. Roman name *VENUS*. Often accompanied by her infant son *EROS*, God of Love, also called *CUPID*.

APOLLO: Greek Sun God, portrayed as a radiant youth; also the God of Poetry and the Arts, often shown carrying a lyre.

ARADIA: Italian Goddess of the Witches.

ARIANRHOD: Celtic Star Goddess.

ATHENA: Greek Goddess of Wisdom, Warfare, and Crafts; depicted in full armor, with shield and spear. Her sacred beasts are owls and spiders. Roman name *MINERVA*.

BAST: Egyptian Cat Goddess; depicted as a cat or a woman with a cat's head.

BRIDE: Celtic Triple Goddess, also known as *BRIGIT*, *BRIGHID,* and *BRIDGET*. Goddess of Poetry, Healing, and Smithcraft.

CERNUNNOS: Celtic horned god. God of the Witches.

CERRIDWEN: Celtic Goddess of Wisdom and Death; associated with sows. Her cauldron contained the brew of bardic inspiration.

DHAGDA: Celtic Father God; depicted with a club and a cooking pot.

DEMETER: Greek Earth Mother. Roman name *CERES*. She went into mourning when her daughter *KORE* was carried off by *HADES*.

DIANA: Roman Goddess of Hunting and the Moon. Greek name *ARTEMIS*.

DIONYSUS: Greek God of Wine and Ecstasy. Roman name *BACCHUS*.

EOSTRE: Germanic Spring Goddess, also called *OSTARA* (origin of the word Easter). Sacred beast: The hare.

EPONA: Celtic Horse Goddess.

FREYA: Nordic Goddess of Love. Friday is her sacred day. Her number is thirteen.

HADES: Greek God of the Underworld. Roman name *PLUTO*.

HECATE: Greek Triple Goddess. Goddess of the Underworld and of Witches; associated with crossroads.

HEL: Nordic Queen of the Underworld.

HERMES: Greek God of Communication, Magic, Medicine, Merchants, Thieves, and Liars. Roman name *MERCURY*.

HERNE: British Stag God, leader of the wild hunt; associated with Windsor

LEFT: *Jackal-headed Anubis escorted the Egyptian dead into the underworld. This wooden mask, with a hinged jaw, would originally have been worn by a priest speaking in the god's name.*

Great Park.

HERTHA: Germanic Earth Goddess.

HORUS: Egyptian Sun God; shown with a falcon's head.

ISIS: Egyptian Great Mother. Later worshiped throughout the Roman world. Wife of *OSIRIS*, mother of *HORUS*.

JANUS: Roman God of Doorways; shown with two faces looking in opposite directions.

JUNO: Roman Great Mother. Married to *JUPITER*. Greek name *HERA*. Sacred beast: The peacock.

LUGH (pronounced *Loo*): Celtic Sun God.

MANNANAN MAC LIR: Celtic Sea God.

MARS: Roman War God. Greek name *ARES*. Lover of *VENUS*.

MORRIGAN: Celtic Goddess of Battlefields and Death. Develops into *MORGAN LE FAY* of Arthurian legend.

NUT: Egyptian Sky Goddess; mated with *GEB*, the Earth God.

ODIN: Nordic All-father. Master of the Runes. Anglo-Saxon name *WODEN*.

PAN: Greek God of the Wild Wood; usually portrayed with cloven hooves, shaggy thighs, horns, and panpipes.

PERSEPHONE/KORE: Kore, Greek Goddess of Spring, was abducted by *HADES* and became Persephone, Queen of the

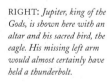

ABOVE: *The Greeks represented their gods as superb physical specimens. This bronze statue of Poseidon was recovered from the sea off Cape Artemision. His trident is missing.*

Underworld. Her myth formed the basis of the eleusinian mysteries. Roman name *PROSERPINA*.

POSEIDON: Greek Sea God; depicted with trident. Roman name *NEPTUNE*.

RA: Egyptian Sun God.

SEKHMET: Egyptian Goddess of Destruction and Healing; depicted as a woman with the head of a lioness. Wife of *PTAH* and mother of *NEFERTEM*.

SIF: Nordic Goddess of the Grasslands; depicted with sickle. Wife of *THOR*.

THOR: Nordic God of Thunder and Industry; depicted with a hammer. Husband of *SIF*.

ZEUS: Greek king of the Gods. Roman name *JUPITER*.

RIGHT: *Jupiter, king of the Gods, is shown here with an altar and his sacred bird, the eagle. His missing left arm would almost certainly have held a thunderbolt.*

The Four Elements

The four elements are earth, air, fire, and water. According to Greek philosopher Empedocles, who lived in fifth century B.C.E., all things animate and inanimate were made up of varying combinations of the four. This was accepted as scientific fact until modern times. Empedocles's theory still makes good psychological and imaginative sense, and Wiccans are happy to work with it. The four elements govern the quarters that make up the circle and are saluted in every ritual.

HUMORS

Air cannot be seen. Fire can be seen but not touched. Water can be touched but not held. Earth can be held. Based on these and other elemental qualities, people were classified into one of four character types. This classification—the theory of humors—was originated by Empedocles.

Earthy people were said to be of a melancholic humor, *fiery* people were choleric, *watery* people were phlegmatic, and *airy* people were sanguine. These terms, now used as adjectives to describe character, were used as technical terms by doctors, philosophers, and other professionals until the nineteenth century.

ABOVE: *The theory of the four elements is essential to prescientific thought. In astrology each sign belongs to one of the four elements.*

RIGHT: *In tarot each suit is governed by one of the four elements—swords by air, wands by fire, cups by water, and pentacles by earth.*

ASTROLOGY

In astrology each sign belongs to one of the four elements: Aquarius, Gemini, and Libra are air signs; Pisces, Cancer, and Scorpio are water signs; Aries, Leo, and Sagittarius are fire signs; and Taurus, Virgo, and Capricorn are earth signs.

ELEMENTAL SPIRITS AND KINGS

In occult tradition a class of spirit belongs to each of the elements. The spirits of air are sylphs, those of fire are salamanders, those of water are undines, and those of earth are gnomes.

Each class of spirit has a king. The king of air is Eurius, usually pictured as a handsome youth. The king of fire is Notus, pictured as a mature man. The king of water is Zephyrus, a middle-aged man, and the king of earth is Boreas, an old man.

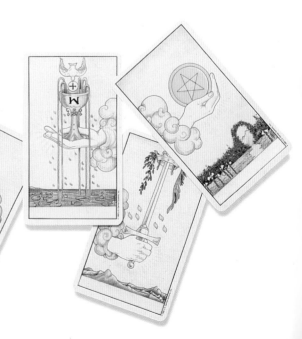

CORRESPONDENCES

Each element is assigned a cardinal point. The usual system is air to the east, fire to the south, water to the west, and earth to the north.

Each element is also assigned a color:

- air—blue
- fire—red, golden, orange, or other sunny color
- water—green
- earth—yellow, black, brown, or other earth tone.

Each element is associated with a Wiccan tool: air is the sword and fire is the wand (these two are often interchanged); water is the chalice, and earth is the pentacle. These symbols correspond to the four suits of the tarot pack—swords, wands, cups, and pentacles.

The list of correspondences is endless. Everything in the universe can be classified as belonging to one of the four elements. An understanding of these correspondences is essential in the practice of magic and spellcraft.

When setting up your Wiccan temple, group objects and symbols belonging to the elements at the appropriate cardinal point, for example:

EAST: incense, joss sticks (or incense sticks), feathers (any kind), wind chimes, fans

SOUTH: extra candles, sun ornaments (in pottery, metalwork, or any other medium), plants (cacti, sunflowers, succulents), a wand

WEST: bowl of water, shells, fish, and/or mermaid ornaments

NORTH: stones, fossils, plants (ivy, aspidistra, hostas), wood, pentacle.

The Fifth Element

The fifth element is spirit and, for Wiccans, it manifests through the other four. It is the breath of life. In order to approach it we personify it in the form of goddesses and gods. In every person there lives an undying spirit. For the Romans, a man's spirit was known as his "genius", a woman's as her "juno." To connect with their juno or genius, Wiccans take a spirit name at initiation.

ABOVE: *The Swiss psychologist Carl Jung (1875–1961) believed the male psyche contained a female component—the "anima"—and the female psyche a male component—the "animus."*

THE SPIRIT NAME

The spirit name you choose to take at initiation can be the name of a goddess or god, of a mythological character, of an animal, tree, or mineral, or even of an appropriate fictional character. The choice of name is linked to what you hope for yourself. For example, a woman who wants to improve her skills in communication could take the name of Iris, Messenger of the Greek goddesses; while a man could take the name of Mercury, Messenger of the Greek gods.

As skills are worked at and mastered, further spirit names are taken. This does not mean that the initiate discards previous identities. It is rather that the old identities are absorbed and become part of the initiate's personality. Once you have taken a god or goddess name, that god or goddess will always be with you.

BEYOND SEX

Spirit is beyond sex. It contains both male and female; the human spirit is androgynous. The Swiss psychologist Carl Jung believed that the male psyche contained a female component known as the *anima* and the female psyche a male component known as the *animus*. In certain circumstances it may be right for an initiate seeking to contact their own *anima* or *animus* to take a spirit name from the opposite sex. This should be done only in exceptional circumstances because the potential for psychological and sexual confusion is considerable. On the other hand, the balancing of male and female energies in the personality is the mark of the truly mature and integrated human being.

THE GREAT SPIRIT

Wiccans call the great spirit *Dryghten*, an Anglo-Saxon word meaning "lord." Use this blessing, invoking Dryghten, to close a Wiccan circle.

66 *In the name of Dryghten the Ancient Providence, which was from the beginning and is for eternity, both male and female, the original source of all things; all knowing, all pervading, all powerful, changeless, and eternal; in the name of Our Lady of the Moon and the Lord of Death and Resurrection; in the names of the Mighty Ones of the four quarters, the Kings of the Elements, we say, blessed be this place and this time and they who are with us. Blessed be.* 99

EXAMPLE SPIRIT NAMES AND MEANINGS

For a man:

MERCURY—communication

HERNE—earth energy

THOTH (or *Spock*)—rational thinking

WOLF—courage

HAWK—clear vision

HERCULES—controlled strength

DIONYSUS—letting go

JANUS—seeing both sides

For a woman:

MINERVA—wisdom

DIANA—independence

IRIS—communication

HAWK—clear vision

WILLOW—resilience

SEKHMET—justified anger

HERTHA—homemaker

TITANIA—self-worth

Healing

In a broad sense healing is about putting things right. One thing that needs healing is our relationship with nature. For many Wiccans, healing the rift between humanity and Mother Nature is the most important work they do. Everyday life damages everyone. Even if we are fit and well physically, psychological damage may need healing. Wiccan ritual attunes us to the cycles of nature and is a healing force.

EARTH HEALING

Wiccans conduct earth-healing rituals. They back these up by doing practical things, ranging from engagement in ecological politics to taking their own litter home and recycling materials. Be sensible about this. If you drive ten miles to recycle three bottles this burns more energy than is saved. Earth healing starts in your own back yard.

If we do not respect our Mother the Earth she will shake us off her back, and life on earth will continue without us.

HEALING OTHERS

Magic is no substitute for medicine, but healing spells and rituals can help. When someone asks you for healing, it is important to ensure that they are also seeking appropriate medical help. If, for example, a woman is asking for help with conception, first make sure that she is in a sexual relationship, and second that she has seen her doctor and is receiving medical help.

In healing, as in all spellcraft, it is essential to be precise about what you want and

HEALING THE SELF

Through initiation we commit ourselves to the exploration of our inner landscape. Here we encounter all those problems that we pushed aside to deal with at another time. In Wicca that time is now. Psychic health depends on change and growth. We sicken when we stay still. The truth you accept as fundamental today may have to be ditched tomorrow when its usefulness has ended. As Mrs. C.F. Alexander, a Victorian poet, wrote:

Not forever by still waters
Would we idly rest and stay
But would smite the living fountains
From the rocks along our way.

how you want to obtain it. Unless you lay out the road map in advance, magic will take the shortest route there is. This could let you or the patient in for a very bumpy ride. For example, a coven was once asked to heal someone suffering with a painful abscess under his arm. A healing spell was cast and the patient pictured as fit and healthy. That night the man was rushed into hospital and operated on immediately. A speedy cure was effected but a little thought might have ensured a gentler, friendlier way of achieving the same result.

HEALING RELATIONSHIPS

No magic should be used in counseling—the manipulation of relationships by magic is almost always a bad idea. The Wiccan operating as priest or priestess should be prepared to listen and be an impartial counselor—but know his or her limitations. Sometimes all it takes to heal a relationship is to have someone willing to listen. However, relationship counseling is a specialized skill, and no one should get into it without knowing what they are doing.

HEXING OR JINXING

Anybody can heal, therefore anybody who can heal can hex or aim to bring misfortune to another. The skilled healer must guard his or her thoughts and take care to illwish no one. Remember—black magic always returns, threefold, to infect and damage the sender.

ABOVE: *Wiccans cultivate ecological awareness. They show respect for the Earth and her resources by recycling where it is possible and reasonable to do so.*

The Wiccan Priesthood

In Wicca there is no distinction between clergy and congregation. All Wiccans belong to the priesthood. Wiccans believe that nobody needs another person to intercede with the gods and goddesses for them. It is one of the aims of Wicca to empower the individual. The Wiccan priesthood is open to women and men, without distinction. The interplay and tension between the sexes is a major source of Wiccan creativity. From the newest priest or priestess to the longest serving high priest or high priestess, all Wiccans are equal.

LEADERSHIP

In practical terms, someone has to run things. If the temple is in your home, you have the right to lay down the basic house rules. Consider yourself to be host priest or priestess. When it comes to teaching, the person with the knowledge takes charge. We all learn from one another. Whoever wants to run a ritual becomes high priest or priestess for its duration.

BELOW: Wicca values the interplay and tension between the sexes. High priestess and high priest are jointly responsible for running the coven; they are assisted by an officer known as the maiden.

WITCH KINGS AND QUEENS

Alex Sanders used to get himself billed as King of the Witches. Whether he crowned himself or was crowned by the media, he embraced the title as a way of getting his message across. He was, apart from everything else, a great showman.

Some Wiccans believe that when you have had four covens hive off, you become Witch King or Queen. As a Witch Queen you get to wear a special garter. If this sort of thing amuses you, then why not? You are not harming anyone, except perhaps yourself, by taking yourself too seriously! Titles have no validity outside the coven that awards them.

Characters who advertise themselves as King or Queen of the Witches (usually with a view to marketing goods) are viewed with skepticism and amusement within the wider Wiccan community.

RESPONSIBILITIES

When you take on the mantle of priest-hood you also acquire an aura of priestliness. Do not be surprised if acquaintances or even complete strangers come to you and start telling you their life stories and problems. They will do this even if they do not actually know you are a priest. It can feel good to be given power to play a part in other peoples' lives—it can also be a burden. Be very careful how you respond.

The Wiccan way is to empower others to sort out their own problems and not to take them over and sort them out yourself. Hand power back to your clients or it will corrupt

ABOVE: *Garters may be decorated with the symbols that appear on the pentacle. Margaret Murray believed that the order of the garter, instituted by Edward III, was originally a witch's coven.*

BELOW: *Wiccans work in a circle, which emphasizes that all are equal. It is customary for men and women to be arranged alternately. This is known as "sitting (or standing) as witches."*

you. Also make sure your skills are up to the job. Do not give counseling unless you are capable. If in doubt, offer support and point people toward appropriately qualified professionals.

As a priest you are likely to be asked for magic. It is easy to get out of your depth. Magic is a tricky and sensitive tool. It has to be handled with intelligence, logic, and clarity. Do not allow your personal feelings to cloud your judgement. Ask yourself whether the thing you are being asked for is really what the person needs. You should never work on a third person without obtaining their consent.

Sacred Space

All space is sacred; the gods and goddesses are present everywhere. The whole earth is a temple. The whole universe is a temple. This, however, is too much for the human mind to comprehend, except in certain mystical states, and from the earliest times we have needed to "rope off" particular areas for worship and ritual. The earliest sacred spaces we can identify are the caves in which our prehistoric ancestors left paintings of themselves and the beasts they hunted.

ABOVE: *Our prehistoric ancestors sometimes used standing stones to mark out sacred space. This is the Long Stone on Shovel Down near Gidleigh, Devon, in England.*

SPIRITS

Sacred space is almost always an enclosure, or an area that is set aside from the everyday world, whether it be a cave, a henge monument with its earthworks and rings of stone, a Greek temple, or a medieval cathedral.

Certain natural features encourage a mood of reverence and contemplation: Hilltops; groves of trees; natural springs; waterfalls; or grand rock formations. Ancient cultures believed that every place, whether grand or humble, possessed an indwelling spirit. The Latin name for such a being is *genius loci*. These spirits might be worshiped as minor deities or honored as nature elementals, like the English faeries or the Irish sidhe (pronounced *shee*).

In the past, generation after generation has been drawn to the same sites. In Europe and throughout the Middle East it is not unusual to find churches and mosques that have been built on the foundations of older Pagan shrines. The Temple Rock in Jerusalem is a fine example of a place that has been sacred to Pagans, Jews, Moslems, and Christians over many thousands of years. The Parthenon in Athens has had a very similar history.

YOUR OWN SACRED SPACE

The world is full of ancestral sacred places. They are places where, to use T.S. Eliot's phrase, "prayer has been valid." Places that have been used for worship over generations may well acquire an atmosphere of sanctity. Depending on the nature of the rites performed in them, they can become welcoming or weird, awe-inspiring or hostile. They can feel haunted. It is good to visit and experience such places, but equally good to create sacred spaces of your own.

IMPROVING THE NEIGHBORHOOD

You do not need to go on a pilgrimage to ancient sites such as Stonehenge in England or Ayers Rock in Australia to find the sacred. The divine is everywhere. Honor the *genius loci* of your own neighborhood. If you live in a run-down inner-city area, then there is all the more reason to honor it and shower it with love. Only by loving a place can we transform it. As G. K. Chesterton said, "If men loved London as men love life, then London would soon be as fair as Florence." By setting up a shrine or temple in your home you are turning it into a holy place.

THE WICCAN CIRCLE

A Wiccan circle is a special kind of sacred space. It is nonphysical, created for a particular purpose and allowed to dissipate after use.

If you want to do magic, it helps to work within a boundary (*see pages 56–57*). The circle concentrates power. It keeps hostile energies out and friendly energies in.

ABOVE: *The modern city can appear inhospitable—all the more reason to see it as a sacred space. Sacredness is not inherent in a site, but is created when human beings honor and love it.*

LEFT: *Hills are frequently regarded as sacred. Glastonbury Tor in Somerset, in England, is believed to be King Arthur's Avalon. In folklore it features as a gateway to the Celtic underworld.*

Setting up a Temple

The goddesses and gods are present everywhere. We do not always notice them, which is why we have a need to create temple space. Your temple can be anywhere you want it to be. It can be temporary or permanent. It need not be anything fancy. Alex Sanders, the charismatic founder of Alexandrian Wicca, had a folding board with a magic circle painted on it which he could open anywhere to create an instant temple; "Have temple, will travel."

RIGHT: *Temple candles should be color-coded: Yellow or brown in the north; blue in the east; red or yellow in the south; and green in the west.*

DEDICATED SPACE

Some Wiccans use their living room as their temple. The coven meet to chat and drink coffee, then, when it is time to begin the ritual, they move the furniture out and set up the temple paraphernalia. Others rent public spaces such as a gym or church hall.

A one-person temple can be set up in a small bedroom; a larger group needs more space. Beware of using your bedroom, unless you enjoy the weird and vivid dreams that this occasions.

A group that used a carpeted cellar found it damp, hard to heat, and they had to watch out for slugs.

PLACING THE ALTAR

Christian churches, Jewish temples, and Islamic Mosques have their altars in the east because that is the direction of the Holy Land and the rising sun.

Wiccan temples always have their altars in the north because Wicca is an earth religion and north is the quarter belonging to the element of earth.

Do not worry if the space you have chosen is not oriented north–south. Simply decide which wall you want to represent the north and put your altar against it.

LEFT: *The altar stands in the north. It serves as a workbench and standing buffet. It needs to be big enough to display the Wiccan tools and the decorations appropriate to the various sabbats.*

ABOVE: *Statues of the gods and goddesses enhance the temple. It would be appropriate to display this statue of Neptune, Roman god of the Sea, in the west.*

DRESSING YOUR TEMPLE

Your altar needs to be big enough for you to display your tools and to have a candle burning. Treat it and its furnishings with respect but try not to get too solemn about them. The Wiccan gods and goddesses have a sense of humor and enjoy puncturing pomposity.

You will also want candles at the other three quarters. Wall sconces (bracket candlesticks) are a good idea. Be conscious of the safety angle and expect to get candlewax on everything. Any carpet you put down in your temple is going to get stained and damaged. Think inexpensive and hard-wearing, but remember you are going to have to sit on it.

Temple candles should be color-coded: yellow, brown, or black in the north; blue or white in the east; red or yellow in the south; and green or blue in the west.

BE CREATIVE

These are the basics. The rest of the furnishings are up to you. Some temples display pictures of the elemental kings at the quarters. An alternative is to have collections of objects associated with the elements. In one temple, for example, there is a wall shelf at west carrying a bowl of water, a figurine of Neptune, a dried starfish, a statuette of a cow drinking from a bucket, various pebbles and shells, a fossil sea anemone, and a little model of a plesiosaur (the long-necked prehistoric marine reptile). The objects you put in your temple are there to help you to focus. Be creative. Be quirky. If you prefer the tranquillity of a plain, uncluttered space with minimal furnishings, then that is excellent too.

LEFT: *Statues are expensive, but shells and stones can be collected from the seashore for free and are also appropriate for display in the west. Be creative in your choice of temple displays. Be quirky.*

Temple Gods and Goddesses

Wiccans develop a close personal relationship with their goddesses and gods, and find their temple gods and goddesses in many different ways. Some say if you choose the goddess she herself will choose the god. Gods and goddesses sometimes present themselves in dreams. Perhaps you already know which of them have chosen you? If not, ask. If you get it wrong, they will keep prodding you until you get it right. They do not give up.

ABOVE: *Epona, Horse Goddess of the ancient Britons, haunted the dreams and meditations of a priestess until the priestess accepted Epona as her spirit name.*

CHOSEN BY EPONA

Sometimes the god or goddess you want for yourself is not the one who wants you. One priestess found that the image of a horse's head kept breaking in on her dreams and meditations. Finally she confronted it and asked for its name. It declared itself to be Epona, Horse Goddess of the Ancient Britons. Up until this point the priestess had been convinced that she belonged to Morrigan, the Irish Goddess of the Battlefield.

YOUR TEMPLE

In order for you to contact your gods and goddesses, you first cast a circle (*see* page 56) and then invite a goddess and god to make themselves known to you. Open your mind, give yourself time, and take a mental note of anything you feel or see or hear. Did you get the impression of a warm, sensual, female pres-

ence? That might be Aphrodite. Did you see a man in a winged helmet? Hermes perhaps. Or a man with a hammer? Thor, maybe. Did you imagine an owl flying in the room or hear one hooting? Owls are sacred to Athena.

THE IMPERSONAL

It is the usual practice to dedicate to a single goddess and a single god, for example, Isis

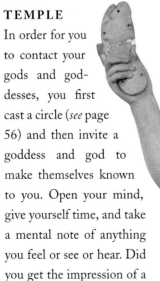

RIGHT: *Invite a goddess and god to make themselves known to you. Open your mind and wait. They may speak to you directly, or through feelings, thoughts, and impressions.*

and Osiris, but the addition of a third dedicatee has much to recommend it. Instead of a straightforward linear interchange of energy, you set up a triangular relationship and the energy has three ways to flow. If you wish to preserve the balance of male and female energies, then pick a third dedicatee who is of neither sex. Possible options are the Full Moon, the Unconquered Sun, and the Morning Star. This choice also acts as a reminder that the divine is beyond personality and sex.

THE POWER OF THREE

Three has always been honored as a number of perfection and completion. The city of Rome was dedicated to the Trinity of Jupiter, Juno, and Minerva. The Egyptians worshiped the holy family of Isis, Osiris, and Horus—mother, father, and child. The Celts

were particularly fond of grouping goddesses and gods in threes. Romans honored the three *Deae Matres* or Mother Goddesses and the three mysterious *Genii Cucullati*, depicted as pixie-like figures in cloaks with hoods.

ABOVE: *Dedication to three deities is especially dynamic. Here the female energy of Juno, and the male energy of Jupiter are balanced and complemented by the asexual power of the Full Moon.*

A SECOND ALTAR

Other gods and goddesses will move in and out of your life. A second altar is an option. This could be dedicated to ones from a different pantheon, or you could set up a miniature altar at each of the quarters. The possibilities to be explored are endless. Work with as many or as few gods and goddesses as you like.

A Witch Alone

In the Gardnerian Book of Shadows *it says: "Ye may not be a witch alone." This is nonsense. The old hedgewitches and cunning-men were almost always solo practitioners. You do not need other people around you to honor the god and goddess, or to practice healing and spellcraft. Many people feel drawn to Wicca but do not want to be part of a group or are unable to find one in their area.*

SOLITARY PRIESTHOOD

The solitary Wiccan has been chosen by the gods and goddesses and is answerable to them alone. Those who work in groups have to compromise. Those who work on their own do not.

As a Wiccan working alone, you are on the path of the Hermit in the Tarot deck. He walks through the darkness. In his lantern burns the Star of Hope and Desire, casting light into lonely places.

In ritual you will call the gods and goddesses down into your circle rather than invoke them into a person; this is known as **evocation**. Because they are not having to function through a human intermediary you will experience their energy in a purer, more elemental form. A very intense rapport builds up between solo practitioners and their gods and goddesses. You and they are alone together.

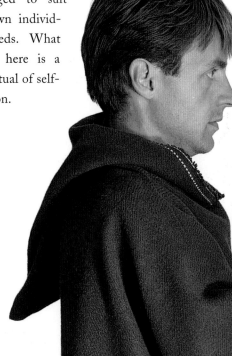

ABOVE: *The Hermit in the Tarot deck, walking alone through darkness, carrying his lantern in which the Star of Hope and Desire burns bright, is the symbol of the solitary Wiccan.*

CONVERTING A RITUAL

The rituals in this book are all written to be performed by a group. Ritual is a group activity. When you work alone, you can be much more informal. You are in the enviable position of not having to please anybody apart from yourself and your gods and goddesses. One way to work the seasonal rituals would be to evoke the gods and then allow their words and interaction to play in your head.

Alternatively, use the words in this book as a basis for meditation, pathworking, and as a gateway into the sabbats. You need to "feel" the sabbat, and allow the temple itself to become your working partner.

The ideas and symbols present in the rituals can be used as building blocks and rearranged to suit your own individual needs. What follows here is a short ritual of self-initiation.

SELF-INITIATION

★ Take into the temple your symbols of first degree: Three cords, each three yards long in red, white, and blue, and a mirror.

★ Place these on the altar.

★ Cast your circle (*see pages 56–57*).

★ Salute the elements (*see pages 76–77*).

★ Kneel before your altar and say:

❝ *(Goddess name) and (god name), Lord and Lady of this temple, I (your name) also known as (your spirit name) kneel before you today (tonight) to ask you to accept me as your priest(ess). I will work no harm and will leave any ill will that I feel outside the temple. Teach me all I need to know. I ask you to guard and guide my life and the work I do for you.* ❞

LEFT: *The initiate looks at their own reflection in the mirror and declares three times to the one who can judge truly: "I am a witch."*

★ Hold up the mirror so that you can see your face in it and say:

❝ *I stand before the one who knows me true and declare:*

I am a Witch.
I am a Witch.
I AM A WITCH. ❞

★ Stand before each quarter and proclaim:

❝ *Brothers and sisters of the (east/south/west/ north), Children of (air/fire/water/earth), I (spirit name) am a witch and priest(ess) of this temple. I ask for your guidance and love. So mote it be.* ❞

★ Close the circle (*see pages 86–87*).

TOP: *At each initiation the Wiccan acquires a different set of colored cords. The colors for the first degree are red, white, and blue.*

ABOVE: *The initiate kneels before the altar and asks the goddess and god to accept him or her as their priest(ess).*

FURTHER INITIATIONS

• Second and third initiations are between you and your gods and goddesses only.

• You do not need a ritual to attain them.

• If you feel you would like a ritual, then make it your second or third degree task to write one.

• Otherwise, simply kneel before your altar, when you feel ready, and ask for what you want.

The Coven

The coven is a Wiccan working group. Members become as close as family—loving, supportive, and sometimes in conflict. It meets on a regular basis. All covens meet on festivals known as sabbats, *and many meet more often. Coven meetings that are not sabbats are known as* esbats. *In fiction covens have a membership of thirteen. In reality it is usually far fewer. Why thirteen? It could be because there are thirteen lunar months to a year. Thirteen is also the number of the houses of the zodiac plus the sun that travels through them.*

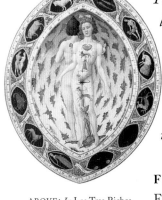

ABOVE: *In* Les Tres Riches Heures *of the Duc de Berry Man stands within a mandala surrounded by the twelve houses of the zodiac. He and they make thirteen.*

FINDING A COVEN

Finding a coven demands determination. Few covens advertise. Subscribe to Pagan magazines, in particular ones local to your area. They will introduce you to the local Pagan scene. One thing leads to another. Often you meet the people you need when you need them. Persevere. You might try surfing the Internet.

SECRECY

In Gardnerian Wicca, emphasis is laid on the need for absolute secrecy about the coven and its membership. This was supposedly a legacy from the days of persecution. These days most Wiccans are a lot more laid back. Even so, caution is advisable. There are still people out there who will persecute you just for being a Wiccan. There are some covens

---

SKY-CLAD

Many covens work *sky-clad* or, in other words, naked. In the Gardnerian *Book of Shadows* it says:

No more shall ye know slavery,
Who give true worship unto me
Ye who tread my round on
Sabbat-Night
Come ye all naked to the rite
In token that ye be truly free.

whose members know one another only by pseudonyms and who do not socialize outside of the covenstead.

LEARNING ENVIRONMENT

The coven is a learning environment. The learning goes both ways. When someone asks for initiation, ask them what they want to get out of Wicca and also what they are bringing to it. Needy and dependent people with nothing to give are not right for coven life. Remember—every member is a priest or priestess, and will be expected to work as one. A coven is too small to carry passengers.

GROUP MINDS

Coven members develop a group mind. Kick one and they all limp. It makes sense not to

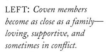

ESBAT INCENSE

Incense should be prepared in advance of a ritual. Charcoal blocks should be lit at the beginning of the ritual and incense scattered on them as required. Incense can be made by mixing together the following ingredients:

- Four teaspoons frankincense tree resin or eight drops of frankincense oil
- Four teaspoons myrrh or nine drops of myrrh oil
- One and a half teaspoons benzoin gum (if using frankincense and/or myrrh oil use half a teaspoon extra for frankincense and one teaspoon extra for myrrh)
- One teaspoon sandalwood resin (use essential oil if unavailable)
- Half a teaspoon orris resin (use essential oil if unavailable)
- Half a teaspoon dried thyme or one tablespoon fresh
- One teaspoon poppy seeds
- Three teaspoons rose petals

LEFT: *Coven members become as close as a family—loving, supportive, and sometimes in conflict.*

initiate anyone you cannot be friends with. It is important that every member of the coven should feel happy with a new initiate. Coven members may find their fellows wandering in and out of their dreams, or linked to them by telepathy. As in all intense relationships, there are no half measures. New initiates begin by hero-worshiping their initiators, move into a phase of doubting them, before finally accepting them as flawed, human beings who are their equals. It is much like the relationship between a growing child and his or her parents. Coven life can be hard but intensely rewarding.

Initiation

Wicca is a mystery religion. When you sign up, you sign up for a transforming experience. You will be taken through the dark recesses of your own being and then reborn into the light. This may happen once or again and again. Wicca is only for those who are strong enough to face their own inner demons. Wiccan groups do not proselytize. If you want initiation, you have to ask. Traditionally a year and a day has to elapse between asking and initiation.

THREE DEGREES

There are three degrees of initiation. Basic teaching will usually be given before first degree. This gives people the chance to back away and change their minds. Some groups keep information and contact in and out of the temple to a minimum before initiation. Others believe the initiate has the right to have some idea of what they are letting themselves in for. The initiator also needs to get to know his or her initiate. It is a good idea to tailor initiation rituals to the individual.

Initiation is between individuals and their gods and goddesses; all a coven can do is admit the person to their working group. Initiation is an inner process that outward ritual merely facilitates.

FIRST DEGREE

First degree is initiation of the personality. It should include an element of ordeal or hazing. The initiate should have no advance knowledge of the contents of the ritual. Wicca is a hard path, and no one should feel too comfortable setting out on it.

The symbol for first degree is a triangle, point downward.

ABOVE: *First degree is the initiation of personality. A woman becomes the goddess and a man becomes god. The symbol of first degree is the downward-pointing triangle.*

At first degree a woman becomes the goddess and a man becomes the god.

SECOND DEGREE

Some people choose not to move beyond first degree. For many people it is enough that they have been initiated and climbing up through the grades is unimportant.

Second degree is initiation of the spirit. It is said to be for this lifetime and all lifetimes to come. This is where the hard work begins. It is often spoken of as the dark night of the

ABOVE: *Second degree is the initiation of the spirit. It is known as the dark night of the soul. The symbol of second degree is the downward-pointing pentacle.*

soul, an underworld journey where certainties disappear. The symbol for second degree is the downward-pointing pentacle.

At second degree the gods and goddesses are internalized by the individual. They are no longer to be found "out there"; they can only be found and experienced within. This is a difficult concept which has to be lived to be understood fully. Some initiates experience this as a devastating loss of faith.

THIRD DEGREE

Third degree returns you to the everyday world. You have emerged from the dark night of the soul. The gods and goddesses are once more there for you, but your relationship with them has changed. Wicca is now as natural as eating and breathing. The externals of the religion fall away and you may find that you no longer need a temple or rituals.

The symbol of third degree is an upward-pointing pentagram piercing a triangle that has a single point uppermost.

At third degree women become the god and men the goddess.

BECOMING AN INITIATOR

When you feel ready to initiate others, go ahead. The gods and goddesses have decided. No words can prepare you for initiation. The experience is wholly personal.

ABOVE: *Third degree returns you to the everyday world. Wicca now comes naturally to you. Its symbol is an upward-pointing pentacle piercing an upward-pointing triangle.*

A TOUCH OF ZEN

A Zen master once described developing spiritual experience in terms of a journey through a natural landscape. The description parallels the experience of Wiccan initiation: "At the beginning of the religious journey a person sees mountains as mountains and trees as trees. In the middle of the religious journey he sees mountains and trees as symbols of an ineffable reality. At the completion of the journey he sees mountains as mountains and trees as trees."

Tools

The working tools of the Wiccan are also known as magical weapons. They consist of a sword, an athame, a white-handled knife, a wand, a pentacle, a censer, a scourge, and the cords of initiation.

SWORD

The sword is used to draw the circle. The idea behind this is that metal is a good conductor of energy. A sword is a good thing to have, but a knife or athame does the job just as well. The use of a sword in Wicca probably derives from ritual magic and freemasonry.

In the days of the witch trials swords were a status symbol, and the sort of people who ended up on the gallows would be unlikely to have had one in their possession.

BELOW:
The athame is a black-handled knife and all-purpose magical tool. The sword is used for drawing the circle. The white-handled knife is used for mundane tasks.

ATHAME

The Gardnerian *Book of Shadows* calls the athame "the true witches' weapon." Any black-handled knife will serve. You do not need a three-foot bowie knife; a folding penknife or decorative letter opener is quite adequate. The athame is used for drawing pentacles, and for drawing the circle if you do not have a sword.

WHITE-HANDLED KNIFE

Traditionally this tool should not leave your temple. It is a practical tool for cutting string, whittling wood, drawing symbols on candles, and other such tasks.

WAND

The wand—a stick about two feet long and decorated to the taste of its owner—is a symbol of magical power. Gardner suggests that the wand might be used in circumstances where sword or athame is inappropriate.

PENTACLE

The pentacle is a round platter or board, which is usually made of wood. If you want to make your own, a cheeseboard or breadboard makes a good blank. It should be decorated with eight symbols, as shown opposite. It is for putting things on which you mean to consecrate.

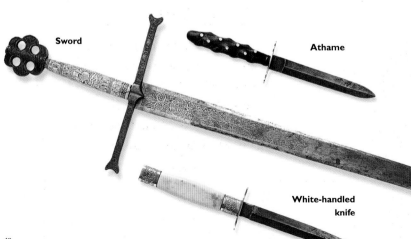

Sword

Athame

White-handled knife

CENSER

The censer is used to burn incense to create atmosphere. A church thurible (a pot on chains) is an ideal vessel. A scallop shell containing sand or a dish of earth are also fine. If you do not wish to fiddle with red-hot charcoal and gummy incense, then joss sticks work just as well.

SCOURGE

Flagellation has been used as a way of altering consciousness for centuries. It was standard practice for the Roman Catholic clergy until recent times. In Gardnerian Wicca the scourge is used as a symbol of female dominance. Many covens find the sadomasochistic overtones distasteful and dispense with it.

CORDS OF INITIATION

Cords are primarily used in initiation. They may be worn in sky-clad rituals as symbols of status. Different covens use different color-coding. Some do not use cords after first-degree initiation. Cords need to be nine feet long, with the ends bound but not knotted. Suggested colors are: **first degree**—red, white and blue; **second degree**—purple and silver; **third degree**—gold.

ABOVE: *The cords are symbols of initiation and achievement. The wand is a symbol of magical authority. The censer is used to burn incense to create atmosphere.*

First Degree

Third Degree

Second Degree

Horned God

Moon Goddess

Scourge

Kiss

USE YOUR FINGERS

Do not get hooked on your tools; they are not indispensable. You can build a circle and work spells without them. Some traditional Wiccans laugh at the use of any kind of tool. "What do you need a knife for when you have fingers?"

The Wheel of the Year

Wiccans visualize the year as a wheel with eight spokes. Each spoke is a major festival or sabbat. *Though some Wiccans count Halloween as their New Year's Day, the wheel, like any circle, has no real beginning and no real end. Any one of the festivals can be treated as a time for endings and new year resolutions.*

RHYTHMS OF NATURE

By celebrating the wheel of the year, which offers a festival every six weeks, Wiccans sharpen their awareness of the changing seasons. The rhythms of nature are easy to ignore in the modern West, where electric lighting takes away the terrors of the winter nights and modern heating banishes the cold. Most of us no longer have to pay attention to the times of sowing and harvest, lambing and culling. The same foodstuffs are there for us in the stores all year round.

For our ancestors it was very different. They had no guarantee that the sun would return to them after its winter decline, and if drought struck or harvests failed they had

BELOW: *The Wiccan wheel of the year has no end and no beginning. It is divided into equal segments by the eight major festivals or sabbats.*

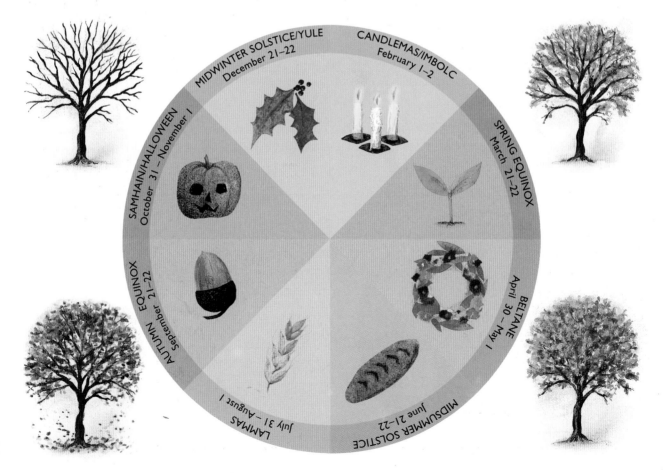

MIDWINTER SOLSTICE/YULE December 21–22

CANDLEMAS/IMBOLC February 1–2

SPRING EQUINOX March 21–22

BELTANE April 30 – May 1

MIDSUMMER SOLSTICE June 21–22

LAMMAS July 31 – August 1

AUTUMN EQUINOX September 21–22

SAMHAIN/HALLOWEEN October 31 – November 1

few resources to fall back on. All ancient cultures paid close attention to the cycle of the seasons, and their monuments often functioned as solar and lunar observatories. For example, at Newgrange in the Republic of Ireland a precisely engineered aperture in the roof of the great mound allows a sunbeam to penetrate an inner chamber at the winter solstice—and only then.

For our ancestors the cosmic drama of seasonal change gave shape and meaning to life. Human hopes were grounded in it. They saw life triumphing over death.

Ancient mythology deals with this drama in terms of gods, goddesses, and heroes. For example, the story of Hercules' Twelve Labors is a parable of the sun's progression through the twelve signs of the zodiac. But Hercules is also one of us. His adventures reflect every man's struggle with adversity. Mythology links individual human life to the life of the cosmos. As above, so below.

ABOVE: *Our ancestors were attuned to the seasons. This sixteenth century painting from the Kalendarium Grimani shows corn being reaped and sheep being sheared in the month of July.*

A WRITTEN RECORD

We no longer share our ancestors' prescientific outlook. By celebrating their festivals we create a bond with them and ensure that we do not take the cycles of nature for granted. Keeping a written record of the seasons year on year is another way of sensitizing yourself. Information about weather and seasonal markers, such as the first spring flowers or the migrations of birds, is an essential part of any magical diary. Wiccans cultivate the attitude which William Wordsworth called "natural piety" in an untitled poem written in 1804:

My heart leaps up when I behold
A rainbow in the sky:
So was it when my life began;
So is it now I am a man;
So be it when I shall grow old,
Or let me die!
The Child is father of the Man;
And I could wish my days to be
Bound each to each by natural piety.

The Waxing Sun

In the season of the waxing sun the light is slowly getting stronger. It is early spring, before we see much change from the dark half of the year to the light. Though a time of hope, it is often hard and grueling.

CANDLEMAS

February is the hardest month. The Yuletide celebrations are a distant memory and the weather remains dark and wintry. Even so, the sun is waxing and the first signs of new life are beginning to appear. For the Romans the whole of February was sacred to Juno Februata, Goddess of Erotic Love. Candlemas celebrates the strengthening light. It announces itself, however implausibly, as the first moon of spring.

Candlemas combines three ancient festivals. The first is Imbolc or Oimelc, a Celtic festival. The second is the festival of Brighid, a Celtic goddess, who, as the Holy Abbess St. Bridget, is the female patron of Ireland. The third is the Christian festival of Candlemas, which commemorates the presentation of the Christ child in the temple.

IMBOLC

In Marsden, a town in Yorkshire, in England, a public celebration of Imbolc is held. A candlelit procession is followed by fireworks and a stylized battle between Jack Frost and Jack-in-the-Green. Children from local schools make and carry lanterns. This festival, devised in the mid-1990s by countryside rangers, shows how the ecological movement draws on pagan and folk traditions.

RIGHT: *The early morning mist rises in the fields that surround the sacred hill at Burrow Mump with its ruined church as spring comes to the Somerset Levels in England.*

Spring Equinox Ritual

In the ritual on pages 90–91 Aphrodite, Greek Goddess of Love, and Dionysus, Greek God of Wine and Ecstasy, are invoked and play out their courtship. The consummation of their love is symbolically enacted in the planting of seeds.

EOSTRE

During the Christian era Easter has been the great spring festival. March 22 is the earliest date on which this movable feast can fall. The spring equinox has, therefore, always been overlaid and muted by the penitential season of Lent and Holy Week.

In the Northern European traditions the spring equinox is also called Ostara in honor of the Saxon goddess Eostre, whose name is perpetuated in the Christian feast. The goddess's feast was celebrated by the giving of colored eggs, symbolizing new life. This is the origin of the modern custom of giving Easter eggs.

LEFT: *Colored eggs which symbolize the gift of new life are exchanged at Easter. The feast derives its name from Eostre, the Saxon Goddess of Spring.*

Imbolc Ritual

In the ritual on pages 88–89 the goddess is invoked as Juno Februata. She moves around the temple lighting candles one by one as a symbol of the return of spring. It is the time for spring-cleaning the temple and for getting rid of personal, spiritual, and psychological baggage.

SPRING EQUINOX

This is celebrated on March 21–22. Day and night are equal; from now on night declines and day lengthens. For the Greeks, March was sacred to Dionysus, God of Wine and Ecstasy, and festivals of plays were held in his honor. For the Romans, March was sacred to Mars, God of War.

The Full of the Sun

Early summer is a time of enterprise. It is the most popular season for marriages. People respond to the freshness of nature by attempting the new and untried. But, for all the apparent brightness, this was an uncanny time for our ancestors. Ghosts and witches were as active at Beltane as at Halloween; Shakespeare's Midsummer Night's Dream, *with its mischievous fairies and bewildered mortals, bears witness to midsummer's reputation as a time of enchantment.*

BELTANE

In the hill country of Northern Europe Beltane was the season when the herds were driven to their summer pastures. In many

ABOVE: *Sixteenth-century peasants celebrate the beginning of summer with feasting, drinking, and a maypole dance in Pieter Brueghel the Younger's vigorous painting of a village kermesse.*

places they were made to pass between two bonfires to rid them of evil influences. Fire was seen as a defense against witches. It is ironic that the witches are now the people who do most to keep the tradition of the Beltane bonfires alive.

Maypoles

Elsewhere the season was celebrated by the young going out into the woods to gather May foliage and blossom. The white foamy blossoms of the hawthorn, or May tree, were particularly prized. It was a time for woodland trysts and mating.

In many places the tradition of erecting maypoles took off. In London's Cornhill district the maypole was taller than the church tower. The resultant nickname stuck, and the church is still known as St. Andrew Undershaft. Young men and women wove around the pole in a pattern which involved much meeting and kissing.

Beltane Ritual

In the ritual on pages 92–93 energy is raised using a verse from Rudyard Kipling's *Puck of Pook's Hill*. Thor and Sif are invoked, a married couple from the Northern European tradition, here representing industry and agriculture. Coven members ask the god and goddess to bless their daily work.

MIDSUMMER SOLSTICE

At midsummer solstice we celebrate the mystical marriage between earth and heaven. God and goddess make love. It is the moment of perfection, but nothing will be as good again. Although the warmest days of summer are still to come, the sun has reached

its zenith and from this point on will be dropping lower in the sky. This is the beginning of the dark half of the year. There is a curious sadness about midsummer. When the sun is at its brightest it casts the deepest shadows.

Solar Calculator and Sun Wheels

The solstice was of great significance in prehistory. Monuments, such as Stonehenge, were laid out as solar calculators, so that its date could be exactly established. These monuments still draw modern Pagans at midsummer. Evidence exists of an ancient ceremony in which sun-shaped wheels were set on fire and rolled down hills. Midsummer was a time for the lighting of bonfires and the holding of fairs.

Midsummer Solstice Ritual

In the ritual on pages 94–95 the British tradition of the bonfire on the hill is conflated with the Greek myth of the death and resurrection of Hercules. Mortally wounded by a poisonous shirt—the gift of a devious

ABOVE: *Stonehenge—one of the most famous prehistoric monuments—is laid out as a solar calculator. It still draws crowds of Pagans, Druids, and revelers at summer solstice.*

LEFT: *"Ne'er cast a clout til t'May is out." Or, in other words, do not take off your winter clothing until the May tree or hawthorn is in bloom.*

enemy—Hercules climbs a mountain and tears up trees to build his own funeral pyre. His living body is consumed by the flames, but his immortal spirit is raised up to heaven by his father Zeus and he becomes a god. Hera, queen of the Gods, who has always seemed to be his foe, welcomes him and gives him her daughter, Hebe, the Goddess of Youth, to be his new bride.

The Waning Sun

Keats's "season of mists and mellow fruitfulness" can be the most beautiful of seasons, as the lazy days of summer change into autumn. The light is amber. The forests turn red and gold. The harvest is gathered in to stock storehouses against the dearth of winter. Homemakers get busy making jams and chutneys, beer and cider.

LAMMAS

Lammas is the time of the grain harvest. The old ballad of John Barleycorn, often used in Wiccan rituals, deals lightheartedly with the great theme of this feast—that transformation comes about through suffering and sacrifice. This is as true of the life of the individual as it is of the barley, which has to be cut and processed to produce "home-brewed ale."

A Wounded Eagle

The word "lammas" derives from the Old English words for "loaf" and "mass"; it describes an old feast day celebrating the first fruits of the harvest. Behind it lies the Celtic festival of Lughnasadh, sacred to the sun god Lugh. A Welsh version of his myth tells how Llew is struck down by his wife, Blodeuwedd and her lover, Gronw, turns into a wounded eagle, and is finally restored to his proper self by the magician Gwydion. The story of Llew can be read as an allegory of the defeat and rebirth of the sun.

Individuation

Lammas is a time for introspection. As Barleycorn and Llew make the journey into the dark in order to achieve transformation, so we look inward in order to grow and change. The individual must stand apart from the group or tribe and know the pain of

ABOVE: *Sunset lights a single ear of wheat and makes it shine like gold. Soon it will be reaped and flayed to be turned into flour.*

RIGHT: *Autumn turns the forest leaves to flame. Beauty goes hand in hand with decay. Sadness is in the air as the world readies itself for winter.*

separation and solitude. As it says in the Gardnerian *Book of Shadows*: "Art willing to suffer to learn?"

Lammas Ritual

In the ritual on pages 96–97 energy is raised using the harvest ballad of John Barleycorn, the Corn God is invoked, and his metamorphosis into bread and beer celebrated.

AUTUMN EQUINOX

At autumn equinox day and night are equal. From this time on, however, the dark grows apace as the nights become longer . It is the season of the fruit harvest. After the pain of Lammas, autumn is a season of mellow light and vibrant color, its sadness balanced by its beauty, as summer comes to an end in an abundance of good things. It is a time for wistful reflection on the transience of life.

Underworld Journey

Wiccans decorate their temples with symbols of autumn, such as pine cones, oak sprigs, acorns, or ears of grain. The ritual often takes the form of a goodbye to the sun. The god is pictured as being on an underworld journey. His vital force is sleeping within the seeds that will come to life in the following spring.

Autumn Equinox Ritual

The Autumn Equinox ritual that is described on pages 98–99 follows an alternative line. The drama of Hades and Persephone is re-enacted. Hades, God of the Underworld, abducts the maiden goddess Kore and she becomes Persephone, queen of the

LEFT: *Corn dollies represent the spirit of the corn. These are buried with the new seeds in spring so that the corn spirit is released back into the field.*

Underworld. Her mother Demeter goes into mourning, and this mourning causes the Earth to become barren. After six months Persephone will be released from the Underworld and spring will arrive once more, bringing new life with it.

BELOW: *Autumn Equinox sees the gathering in of fruit. Wiccans load their altars with fruit as a thanks-offering to the goddess and god of the harvest.*

The Dark of the Sun

The winter months were a time of anxiety for our ancestors. It was a season to be endured and survived. To keep their spirits up, they studded the dark with festivals. In many cultures the feasting at the midwinter solstice went on for days or weeks. Many of the ancient feasts, such as Lammas, have faded in modern times, but Halloween, Thanksgiving, and Yule remain as strong as ever.

HALLOWEEN

Halloween and Beltane were both feared as times when "the veil between the worlds" was thin. People took precautions against witches and evil spirits. Beltane has now largely lost its uncanny reputation, leaving Halloween as the yearly celebration of "ghoulies and ghosties and long-legged beasties and things that go bump in the night."

In popular thought uncanny Halloween is the Wiccans' festival par excellence. This is not really the case. For Wiccans, Halloween is no more important than the other seven festivals.

BELOW: *In many cultures the feasting around the midwinter solstice went on for days. Here an aristocratic family make merry in a painting from the Luttrell Psalter circa 1340.*

SAMHAIN

In Ireland Halloween was the festival of Samhain, when kings and warlords gathered their subjects for sports and feasting. It was a time when the herds would be culled to make the winter fodder go further.

In Christian times Samhain became the feast of All Saints, or All Hallows, a day when the dead heroes of the Christian faith were commemorated.

Samhain Ritual

In the ritual on pages 100–101 the god is invoked as Gwyn ab Nud, British Lord of the

YGGDRASIL

Wiccans deck their houses with holly and ivy and feast like many others at this time of year. This is what the Romans did, and the Norsemen too. After cakes and wine, presents are exchanged. Some covens believe that presents should be made and not bought. The Christmas tree is a reminder of Yggdrasil, the world tree, upon which Odin hung in the ordeal that won him the runes.

Underworld, whose palace was supposedly sited under Glastonbury Tor. The goddess is evoked as Epona, Horse Goddess of the Celtic people, and she is asked to protect the circle and those in it from mischievous spirits. A visualized doorway is cut between this world and the world of the ancestors.

YULE: THE MIDWINTER SOLSTICE

Yule is the midwinter solstice, the longest night of the year. A festival of lights and feasting is more or less a psychological necessity. All the ancient European cultures celebrated at this time. The modern Christmas celebration is a mixture of ancient custom and Victorian sentiment.

Yule ushers in the light half of the year. The Great Mother gives birth to the Child of Hope. In Middle Eastern temples, centuries before Christianity, priests would emerge from the inner sanctum at midnight and proclaim "The Virgin has borne a child. The light is waxing." The New Testament nativity stories simply recast the age-old imagery of the sun god's rebirth. In Egyptian art the images of Isis with Horus on her knee are almost indistinguishable from those of the Madonna and Child.

Midwinter Solstice Ritual

In the ritual on pages 102–103 prayer is made to Isis, Queen of Heaven, for the return of the light. A priestess is invoked as Isis and a priest is invoked as Horus. A veil, symbolizing the darkness of winter, is lifted to dramatize the god's return in strength.

ABOVE: *Wiccans deck their houses with holly and ivy and feast like many others during the winter solstice.*

2 Preparation for Ritual

Make sure that everyone knows their responsibilities before the ritual begins. It is normal for the high priest to be in charge of preparing the temple and the high priestess to be in charge of running the ritual.

Shower or bathe before a ritual. Think of yourself washing away the grime of everyday living in preparation for a walk between the worlds. Put on clean clothes and your circle jewelry and perfume, if worn. It is normal not to put on ritual clothing until just before the ritual. Don't sit around drinking coffee skyclad or wearing your ceremonial robes.

If you are working with a group make sure that it is functioning as a group. Some covens have an elaborate hierarchy of coven officers; others do not. Allow an hour or more between people arriving and the beginning of your ritual. You need time to relax together and allow the group mind to reestablish itself. Any tensions or serious problems need to be acknowledged and, if they cannot be sorted out, set aside before the ritual begins. Within the circle you must work with perfect love and perfect trust.

It is easier to work magic if you have not had a heavy meal. Also, feasting is part of the ritual, so it is good to go into the event with an appetite.

Spend the latter part of your relaxation time discussing the purpose of the ritual. If people want to perform spells, this is the time to decide whether and how the spell is to be done. On occasion it is a good idea to ask someone in the group to give a talk or lead a workshop on a relevant subject.

If you are working alone, allow yourself time to relax, reflect on any problems, and set aside the mundane before you start.

Do not worry if you are not in the right mood. Sometimes the best rituals happen when you feel least like doing them.

Opening the Circle

The ritual for opening a circle remains much the same no matter what follows. The only variation is the wording of the opening invocation. The text of the opening ritual is in Chapter 3, pages 74–75.

CHECKLIST

Before starting a ritual, make sure you have the following:

- Candles
- Incense
- Charcoal
- Incense burner (or joss sticks and holder)
- Matches or lighter
- Cakes and wine
- Bottle-opener
- Athame
- Sword
- Water
- Salt
- Flowers or other decoration for the altar.

BEFORE YOU START

★ Make sure your temple is fully equipped (*see Checklist, left*).

★ Lock outer doors.

★ Turn off all phones and leave cell phones outside the circle.

★ Leave watches outside the circle (ritual time—known as Wiccan Standard Time —is very different from clock time).

BUILDING THE CIRCLE

Although we call it a circle, the space you are building is actually a sphere. You are creating a space between the worlds (ours and that of the goddesses and gods).

You build it layer by layer using each of the four elements, seal its existence with the sword, and then ask the divine to fill it with light. The fifth element, of spirit, you pro-

---

ESBAT/SABBAT PROGRAM

An esbat or sabbat from start to finish is made up of the following:

- Opening the circle
- Saluting the elements
- Energy raising
- Invoking/Evoking the god and goddess
- Charging/Communing with the god and goddess
- Interplay (if any) between god and goddess and/or the people
- Spells and healing
- Cakes and wine (the Great Rite)
- Chanting, dancing, musicmaking, games (optional)
- Feasting and socializing
- Closing or expanding the circle

NOTES

- It is customary for men and women to stand or sit alternately. All movement in the circle, unless otherwise stated, should be sunwise. In the northern hemisphere this is clockwise (deosil); in the southern it is counterclockwise (widdershins).
- The athame and sword are used as conduits for the priest's or priestess's own energy. Picture the energy coursing down the blade.

vide yourself. The circle is a microcosm, a miniature universe.

While building the circle, visualize the space it contains as an island. With salt and water you create the land and sea. With incense you are adding the air and the sun.

MUSIC

Music is not strictly necessary, but it does help to set the mood. If you have musicians in the group, encourage them to work on music appropriate to ritual. Otherwise use music on tape or CD. It needs to be in the background, creating an ambience without drawing attention to itself. Avoid anything with strong vocals. New Age meditation music is ideal.

SWEEPING THE CIRCLE

Yes, witches do possess broomsticks! You are going to need one now to sweep the circle. A traditional besom—a broom made of twigs tied to a handle—is best. The noise this makes, not unlike the sound of the sea, will ease you into a magical frame of mind. Sweep slowly, with long strokes, moving sunwise.

OPENING INVOCATION

The opening invocation is your statement of intent. It can be as simple or as elaborate as you like. You will find examples at the beginning of each of the rituals in Chapter 3.

SALT AND WATER

★ A priest and priestess stand in front of the altar facing one another.
★ The priest takes the bowl of water from the west.

★ The priestess draws a pentagram in the water with her athame and says the words of consecration.
★ He puts the bowl on the altar.
★ The priestess picks up the bowl of salt.
★ The priest draws a pentagram in it and says the words of consecration.
★ He then passes the salt to the priestess and holds the bowl of water for her to add the salt.
★ She stirs the salt and water together, saying the appropriate words.
★ She anoints his forehead with the water.
★ Each consecration is sealed with a kiss.
★ She then does the same for any other priests.
★ He takes the bowl and anoints her and the other priestesses.
★ She takes the bowl and walks around the circle, sprinkling water.
★ The bowl is then returned to the west.

BELOW: *A priest sweeps the periphery of the circle with a* besom *(traditional broomstick). The sound, not unlike the sound of the sea, generates a magical frame of mind in coven members.*

57

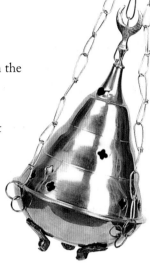

CENSER

★ The priestess takes the censer from the east and passes it to the priest.

★ He says the words of consecration.

★ He wafts smoke at her, and then at the other priestesses.

★ She then does the same with the priests.

★ He walks around the circle, slowly, carrying the censer.

★ The censer is then returned to the east.

ABOVE: *Participants in the ritual are consecrated with the aromatic smoke from the censer. A priest then carries the censer around the circle to consecrate it.*

SWORD

★ The priest kneels and holds the sword out to the priestess.

★ She takes it and, holding it about waist-height, walks

LEFT: *A priest passes the sword to a priestess, who then draws the magic circle by walking round with the sword held out at waist height.*

around the circle saying the words (*see pages 74–75*).

★ She visualizes light passing down her arm, into the sword and so forming the circle.

★ She returns the sword to him.

CANDLE

★ The priestess takes a burning candle from the altar and hands it to the priest.

★ The priest walks around the circle saying the words (see page 75), and sealing the circle, imagining the space to be filled with white light.

CUTTING A DOORWAY

Once you have set up a circle do not breach it lightly. You risk destroying all your hard work. If you have to leave the circle, do the following:

★ Stand facing the door of the room.

★ Close your eyes and feel, with your athame, for the sword-line used to draw the circle.

★ When you have found it, imagine that you are lifting the line (as you would a rope) with the point of your knife.

★ Cut the shape of a doorway, moving widdershins.

★ Place your athame across the threshold.

★ Step through.

★ When you return, pick up your athame and simply redraw the sword-line across the area you have breached, working deosil.

Note: *Animals do not breach a circle and can move in and out with impunity.*

SALUTING THE ELEMENTS

To complete the opening of the circle you need to salute the four elements. In the first ritual on pages 76–77, they are addressed democratically as brothers and sisters. Some Wiccans prefer to deal with each quarter as a kingdom, ruled over by an elemental king. King of the east is Eurius, who is visualized as a handsome youth. King of the south is Notus, visualized as a dynamic young man. King of the west is Zephyrus, visualized as a middle-aged man. King of the north is Boreas, who is seen as an old man. These are the Greek names for the four winds.

To salute the elements:

★ Stand in front of each in turn (starting with the east).

★ Draw the appropriate invoking pentagram (*see below*) with your athame.

★ Say the greeting and call up a mental image of the element.

What you visualize is up to you. You may want to imagine the elemental kings, but do not be alarmed if the picture that presents itself is surprising. Zephyrus, in particular, is something of a comedian. One priestess always sees him as a happy drunk with a cup in his hand. Another sees him as a cheerful fisherman wearing bright yellow oilskins and matching sou'wester.

Alternatively you could call up representative pictures from nature, for example:

- a cloudy sky for the east
- a desert sun for the south
- a breaking wave for the west
- a rocky hilltop for the north.

Try to *feel* what you are visualizing— engage your imagination and all your senses. If you are facing the west, feel the spray on your face and taste the salt.

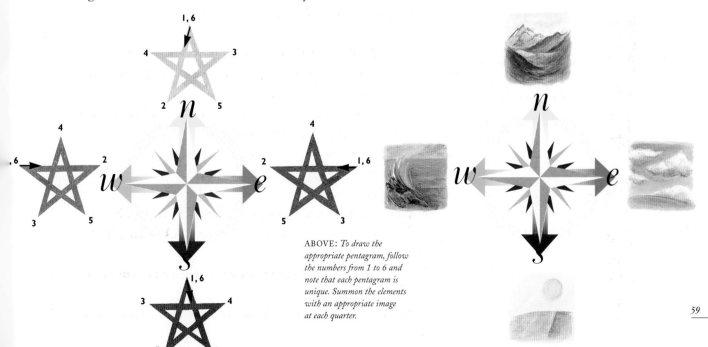

ABOVE: *To draw the appropriate pentagram, follow the numbers from 1 to 6 and note that each pentagram is unique. Summon the elements with an appropriate image at each quarter.*

Raising Energy

After opening the circle, you need to "raise energy." Energies are raised in ritual through intense physical activity, usually a circle dance, or through mental activity, as in the exercise called Roots and Branches (see page 79), or by pulsing energy from person to person, as detailed below. The circle stops the raised energies from escaping. The energies are concentrated into a "cone of power"; this acts as a bank from which we make withdrawals of energy to facilitate magic.

THE CIRCLE DANCE

★ A cauldron is placed in the center of the floor.

★ If it is safe to do so, put a small amount of fuel in the cauldron and ignite it. Otherwise, stand a lit candle in it.

★ Dancers link hands, with the sexes alternating. This is known as "standing as witches."

★ The high priestess begins the chant.

★ The dancers move deosil, slowly at first, then picking up speed.

★ As you dance, you build the cone of power. In your mind's eye visualize a line of energy coming from each person and forming a rising cone in the center of the circle, point uppermost.

★ When the high priestess feels the cone to be complete (some people will actually "see" it as complete), she brings the chant to a climax.

★ Everyone halts and raises their arms.

★ Everyone lowers their arms slowly, to steady the cone. It will expand to fill the temple and energize everyone in it.

★ This is sealed by the high priestess saying "so mote it be."

Note: Some people say that the traditional pointed witch's hat is a symbol of the circle and cone of power. The brim of the hat is the dancing people, the crown of the hat is the cone.

CHANTING

Chants do not need tunes, but do have to have a good regular beat. Almost anything will do. An excellent mantra-like chant can be made out of god names. Folksongs such as *John Barleycorn* can be used (see page 78 for full text), as can some pop songs. They do not have to be highly serious. If everyone bursts out laughing, that raises energy too. A favorite chant for high summer is *The Sun Has Got His Hat On*. Poems in regular meters are also suitable. The chant printed in the Beltane ritual on page 92 is extracted from a longer poem by Rudyard Kipling. If all else fails, try making up your own.

MENTAL ENERGY

If there are only a couple of you, then whirling around in a circle holding hands will only make you sick and dizzy. Another way of raising energy is to pulse it from person to person. This is done as follows:

★ Hold hands with right palm up and left palm down.

ABOVE: *The traditional witch's hat is said to be a symbol of the cone of power. The brim is the dancing people and the crown of the hat is the cone of energy.*

★ Visualize energy coursing through your body and send it out by squeezing hands.

★ This goes around the circle, deosil, faster and faster until you have built the cone of power.

A gentle way of raising energy is through the mental exercise known as Roots and Branches (see pages 78-79). In this exercise you draw both earth energy and sky energy into yourself and focus it into the cone of power.

RIGHT: *If there are only a couple of people in the circle, a good way of raising energy is to pulse it from person to person by squeezing hands.*

BELOW: *The circle dance is an age-old method of raising energy. The dancers move sunwise around a lit cauldron with men and women spaced alternately.*

Drawing Down the Moon

In Wiccan ritual we meet goddess and god directly. A priestess is invoked as the goddess—she becomes the goddess and speaks the goddess's words. This is known as "drawing down the moon." A priest is invoked as the god—"drawing down the sun." In elaborate rituals there may be dialogue between goddess and god or the enactment of a mythic drama. Invocation can have a life-changing effect. Gods or goddesses are always with you once you have embodied them.

PROJECTING ENERGY

There is no rule as to whether goddess or god is invoked first. On occasion one is invoked but not the other.

★ The person being invoked should be in a receptive frame of mind.

★ He or she should stand in front of the altar in the "god position"—arms crossed and hands resting against the shoulders.

★ The invoker kneels at their feet. The invoker needs to have a clear picture in their mind's eye of the god or goddess being called down.

★ The invoker then projects this image onto the other person.

★ The invoker also projects energy. This is drawn from the energy that has already been raised within the temple. Imagine it as a flexible beam of light that is wound in a spiral around the person being invoked, from their feet to the crown of their head. The other people in the temple should help by sending energy to the invoker.

THE WORDS OF INVOCATION

While the invoker is doing these things they speak the words of invocation. The invocation describes the god or goddess in words and asks them to manifest. These words may be improvised or scripted. If you are working from a script, learn it by heart. Your intent will be weakened if you are fiddling with a bit of paper. Sample invocations can be found in Chapter 3.

★ When the invoker has finished, they send a final surge of energy to seal the divine image upon the person being invoked.

★ The invoker sits back with bowed head and waits.

★ Now everybody else needs to be receptive.

★ The god or goddess is about to speak.

RIGHT: *A priestess prepares to be invoked by standing in the god position, with arms crossed, hands resting against the shoulders, and in a receptive frame of mind.*

A GOD IN A WHEELCHAIR

The person being invoked does not have to resemble their god or goddess; this is about who you are on the inside, not about how you look. For example, to be invoked as a Mother Goddess, a woman does not need to have children. A man in a wheelchair can be invoked as a dancing Dionysus. Invocation is partly about trying on new personae and extending your emotional range.

ABOVE: *The invoker needs to have a clear picture in their mind of the deity who is being asked to manifest and must be able to put this into words.*

Invocation can be used to explore underused parts of your personality or to lay claim to qualities you need. A man who is overly intellectual might gain a great deal from being invoked as an earthy, instinctual god such as Pan. A woman who needs to be more assertive might choose to be invoked as Athena the Warrior Maiden or Sekhmet the rampaging Lioness Goddess of Egyptian Memphis.

Charging

When a god or goddess has been invoked in a coven member, that person is infused with energy that is then shared with the other members. The person invoked speaks as the god or goddess; this is called charging.

★ You are standing in front of the altar and your companion is projecting the divine force toward you.

★ Be receptive. As far as is possible, clear your mind of preconceived ideas. Listen to what is said.

★ Allow the energy to envelop you.

★ You become the god or goddess but you remain yourself as well.

★ You are not being possessed. You are allowing the god or goddess to merge with you, and to speak through you, but not handing over complete control.

HOW WAS IT FOR YOU?

Experience what it feels like to be the god or goddess. What are you wearing? Are you holding anything? What is your state of mind? Do you feel benevolent or angry? What do you want to say to the people in front of you? Be prepared for surprises. Gods and goddesses do not always conform to the image you have of them. One priestess, who was invoked as Paachi-Mama, a South American goddess, expected a mature sensual woman to turn up. Instead she got a shy, prepubescent girl, who looked around and said: "Yes, this is nice, I like it here." Paachi-Mama has remained with the priestess ever since.

THE CHARGE

★ Once you feel the god or goddess settled upon you, open your arms wide, in what

RIGHT: *The priestess who has been invoked spreads her arms wide, in what is known as the "goddess" position and speaks the words of the goddess to her people.*

is known as the "goddess position," and radiate the divine energy to all those in the temple.

★ Then speak. The words you speak are known as the charge.

★ You may have a charge ready prepared. If you have, speak it from memory—do not read it from a piece of paper.

If you have the confidence to improvise your charge, so much the better. A preprepared charge can cause you to lose the divine energy in two different ways:

• First, it tends to run through your mind when you are being invoked and block the invocation

• Second, you have already pre-empted what the god or goddess will say.

Improvisation permits you and the god or goddess to be responsive to the moment. The best charges are those that take everyone, yourself included, by surprise.

Do not worry too much about the words. Indeed, you do not have to say anything— radiating the presence of the divine is enough. Sometimes the gods and goddesses themselves have nothing to say.

EARTHING

★ When your charge is finished, drop your hands to your sides.

★ If there is no more interplay between god and goddess, this will give your invoker the cue to "earth" you.

★ This is done by the woman standing with her toes on top of the man's feet,

ABOVE: *After she has charged, the priestess is "earthed" by an embrace from her invoker. She places her toes on his feet, to make a circle, and they kiss.*

thus making a circle.

★ They embrace and kiss.

★ Holding on to the energy too long can be dangerously disorienting. You need to return to yourself.

SEXUAL POLITICS

The encounter, between invoker and invoked, can be intense. Both should be aware of the sexual politics involved. The invoked priest or priestess should not exploit the divine energy for sexual grati-fication. There must be courtesy and respect on both sides. If those involved are already lovers, there should not be a problem. Be careful, however: You should not let the god or goddess energy lead you into something you will regret later.

WORKING ALONE

The solitary witch, after evoking his or her god or goddess, should listen, relax, and commune with the divine energy.

RIGHT: *Cakes and wine are blessed and passed around the group when all the work has been done. Then the feasting can begin.*

The Great Rite

The "Great Rite" is Gardner's rather coy term for making love as the climax of ritual. The coyness is understandable when you remember that he was writing in the 1950s when D.H. Lawrence's Lady Chatterley's Lover *was still banned in the United Kingdom. For Wiccans, sexuality has always been as natural and holy as it was for our Pagan ancestors. Christianity banished sexuality from religion. This has had a crippling effect on Western society. Gardner, like Lawrence and other pioneers, set out to right this wrong. In Wicca sexual intercourse is reinstated as the archetypal creative act and the heart of true religion.*

DIVINE SEXUALITY

Ancient mythology is always sexually frank. The old gods and goddesses are all sexual beings. In Greek myth their sexual intrigues and adventures helped shape the world and its history, for example the barrenness of the winter months is accounted for by Hades' abduction of Peresphone, the Spring Maiden. On the painted ceilings of the royal tombs of Egypt, the star-filled body of Nut the Sky goddess arches over that of the ithyphallic Earth god Geb. Their lovemaking creates and sustains the visible universe.

ACTUALITY

The Great Rite may be performed either in actuality or symbolically. In practice the actual Great Rite is performed only in private between partners who are already lovers. The priest and priestess should first invoke one another as goddess and god and both should charge. It makes sense for the goddess and god to be compatible: Herne and Aradia are a natural couple, so are Mars and Venus and Isis and Osiris. Be wary of invoking a goddess such as Diana who maintained an image of chastity while

BELOW: *When performing the "Great Rite," priest and priestess should be invoked as compatible deities. Mars and Venus, depicted here by Botticelli, make a good match.*

taking human lovers on the sly. Gods whose sexuality is complicated could cause you problems. Fastidious Diana, for example, would not take kindly to being partnered with undiscriminating Pan.

★ When enacting the Great Rite, one partner lies on the floor, in the center of the temple, arms and legs outstretched, forming a pentacle.

★ The other kneels in front of them, between their feet and says:

66 *Foot to foot (kisses the feet), knee to knee (kisses the knees), phallus to womb (kisses base of stomach), breast to breast (kisses breasts), lips to lips (kisses lips).* 99

★ They then move into the Great Rite. Alternatively, they can exchange the following dialogue before lovemaking:

ABOVE: *A priestess lies in the pentacle position, with arms and legs outstretched. A priest kneels between her feet and together they perform the "Great Rite."*

Person 1: *"Key to lock"*
Person 2: *"And the gate opens"*
Person 1: *"Rain to earth"*
Person 2: *"And the garden blossoms"*
Person 1: *"Breast to breast"*
Person 2: *"And the dance begins"*

SYMBOLICALLY

In public ritual the Great Rite becomes a symbolic action using cakes and wine (*see* page 86). The athame held by the priestess represents the phallus; the wine cup held by the priest represents the womb.

CONSECRATING TEMPLES

A performance of the Great Rite is the ideal way of consecrating a temple. At orgasm the couple should visualize the released energy flooding out to fill and enliven the temple space.

Making Magic

Wiccan magic flows out of Wiccan religion. The energy raised during a ritual will, if left to itself, dissipate into the environment. Rather than allow the energy to go to waste, Wiccans use it for healing and empowerment. The point of spells is to change or adapt reality in line with the magician's will. Before you tackle any spell, be sure that your motives are pure and that your object is both achievable and desirable. Changing reality is not something that should be done lightly or frivolously. Be careful what you ask for—you may get it!

SPELLS

Spells are serious matters. The best time for the casting of spells is after the invocations and charges. Try to prioritize. The first spell you do is likely to use up a lion's share of the available energy. Try not to wear yourself out; three spells will be enough for any ritual. Plan out your spells before you go into the temple.

OTHER MAGICAL SKILLS

Apart from casting magic spells, you may want to exercise other magical or quasi-magical skills before the ritual finally winds down in feasting.

Most Wiccans work at developing one or other of the divinatory arts—now is the time to get out your tarot pack, black mirror or bag of rune stones.

BELOW: *Tarot can be traced all the way back to the Middle Ages. The runes developed in northern Europe, where they were revered as the gift of the god Odin.*

BE SENSITIVE

Magic is a way of manifesting the gods and goddesses on the physical plane. In making magic Wiccans will do nothing that transgresses the Wiccan Rede. When making magic within a ritual ensure the spell is suited to the season and to the atmosphere. Halloween—with its dark energies—is probably not a time for healing spells. Be sensitive to time and place. Some Wiccans time their magic by the moon. Waxing and full moon are for giving; waning and dark of the moon are for taking away.

Be sensitive about the gods and goddesses you are working with. If in your ritual you have invoked a Greenwood God (a god of the forest or wood), there may be little point in doing a spell to clear a fungal infection; he will think they are wonderful. If you are doing a spell to help someone pass an exam, an erudite god such as Hermes will be sympathetic, while a nature god such as Pan will be unlikely to see the point.

MAGICAL ALLIES

The four elements are your magical allies. Call on them when you need to. A woman wanting help with study devised a spell invoking the element of air. A man lacking in pragmatism enlisted the help of the element of earth by consecrating a flint in the circle and wearing it around his neck.

Much of what you do, especially in healing, is about restoring balance. A person seeking help to reorder his or her life might be taken around the quarters and consecrated in turn with air, fire, water, and earth.

ABOVE: *The moon's energy reinforces Wiccan magic. The waxing and full moon are for giving; the waning and dark moon are for taking away.*

SPELL FOR PERSONAL EMPOWERMENT

★ Focus desire for empowerment in a yellow candle. Light the candle and say:

"Mighty and Gentle Lord and Lady,
Whose loving gives me life,
Inspire me to dream great dreams
And give me the strength to make them real."

EARTH HEALING SPELL

★ Stand in the correct quarter (preferably outside), picture the pollution above and around you. As you say "begone," picture it dispersing.

East: *"Pollution of the Air, begone. Scatter on the wind, thinner and thinner, until you can do no harm."*

South: *"Great Sun, gentle your rays; give life-giving fire and harm us not."*

West: *"Pollution of the Water, begone. Let the seas dilute you until you can do us no harm."*

North: *"Pollution of the Land, begone. Drain through the Earth, weaker and weaker, until you can do no harm. So mote it be."*

Back to Earth

Once all the work has been done, cakes and wine are blessed (see pages 84-85) and passed around the group. Then the feasting begins. This time of feasting is as important as anything that has gone before. It helps everybody to return to "normal." It is a time for socializing, bonding, and having fun. Gossip is allowed but malicious gossip in a circle is dangerous; after all, the gods and goddesses are listening in. Humor is the best way that there is to dissipate disturbing energies. Eating and drinking are the best ways of bringing a person back down to earth.

TOASTING THE GODS

Some covens expect a financial subscription from their members. Out of this the host priestess provides the feast. Others ask everyone to bring food and drink. Someone generally needs to coordinate this, otherwise the group mind kicks in and everyone turns up with the same things.

A good game involves each person toasting a god and goddess (not necessarily a couple) before they drink. If they cannot think of any they forfeit a drink. The divine is in everyone, so toasting Homer and Marge or Mulder and Scully, or even Homer and Scully is acceptable.

A CAUTIONARY TALE

It is foolhardy to let anyone drive immediately after a ritual, especially when they have had the goddess or god energy called down upon them. You need to make sure that they are fully "earthed" before they leave.

Folklore tells of a young man who, having been invoked as Herne at a midsummer rit-

ABOVE: *As the cup goes around the circle sunwise, each person toasts a goddess and god. This is Jupiter. Who would you pair him with?*

LEFT: *Cakes and wine are only the beginning of the feast. If you have worked fasting, you will want to follow your ritual with a celebratory meal.*

ual, set off home soon afterward on his motorbike. He was found by the police after midnight in a park at the center of an English city; he was charging around— totally naked—believing himself to be a stag.

CLOSING A CIRCLE

Many Wiccans have a ritual for closing a circle. They start with the blessing prayer and then "unmake" the circle piece by piece.

A small portion of the cakes and wine is kept for a libation (a ceremonial sharing of food and drink with the gods and goddesses). Crumble the cake and pour wine onto the earth while saying a few words, thanking the gods and goddesses of nature.

Finally the following traditional statement is used to end the ritual before leaving the temple:

"Merry meet, merry part, and merry meet again."

BELOW: *To banish the pentagrams, follow the numbers from 1 to 6 and note that each pentagram is unique. Imagine the energy being drawn back into your athame.*

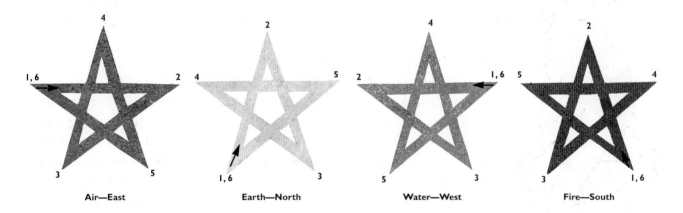

Air—East Earth—North Water—West Fire—South

This is done by "banishing" the representatives of the four elements—by drawing the appropriate banishing pentagram and telling them to return to their "fair and lovely realms." This is sometimes followed by the "undrawing" of the circle—taking the sword around the circle widdershins.

Others feel it is unfriendly and impolite to tell the goddesses, gods, and quarters to leave because they are finished with, and better to allow them to go in their own good time. They are guests, not employees. Instead of banishing, they say the blessing prayer and visualize the circle expanding to fill the whole house and yard.

LEFT: *After the ritual crumble a small portion of cake and pour a little wine onto the earth as a libation or thank-offering to the gods and goddesses of nature.*

3 | Getting Started

This chapter contains specimen rituals that can be used at any esbat, rituals for the eight sabbats, and a set of rituals for first, second, and third degree initiation. You can use them as they stand or adapt them to your own requirements. All except the initiations can be worked by one person on their own. You will also find information on how to cast spells and some useful examples and, in Pathworking, a guided visualization exercise.

If you are working solo it is better, and safer, to call the gods into the circle rather than to invoke them upon yourself. This is known as evocation (see pages 82–85). Evocation takes longer than invocation. Give yourself time to build the picture of the god and goddess you are evoking. Once you have built the picture spend time communing with them. If you speak to them, they may very well answer.

When the ritual has finished, release the god and goddess by saying:

> (God and/or goddess) I thank you for your presence here, and the help you have given me. I ask for your blessing and, ere you depart for your fair and lovely realm, I do bid you hail and farewell.

In ritual you work with invisible forces. In order to make them "real" you need to see them in your mind's eye. The making of mental images is known as visualization. It is an essential magical skill. In ritual and spell-casting you will find that you often have to form mental images of all sorts of things. If this is new to you, do not panic. It is something that we all do in everyday life without thinking about it. We do it when we daydream. We do it when we read novels. Most people when they talk on the phone "see" the person at the other end of the line. Try not to worry if you feel that your visualization skills are not brilliant. One competent high priestess confessed all she sees in visualization are stick people. Practice hones visualization skills.

An Opening Ritual

To create your own sacred space in your temple, follow the suggested plan below. Before you begin, read the instructions in Opening the Circle *on pages 56–59.*

★ Sweep the circle.

★ Speak the opening invocation:

Priest(ess): 66 Let us honor the Powers of Life and Death. Let us be for them as they are for us, holding their love in our hearts. Let us show respect for all that is, for all in Nature has beauty and worth. 99

All: 66 Blessed be. 99

★ Consecrate the water, saying:

66 Water, first home and sustainer of life, be clear of all impurity. Purify us as you are pure, in the name of the goddesses and gods. 99

★ Consecrate the salt, saying:

66 Salt, incorruptible earth of the gods, bonding us as brothers and sisters, purify us as you are pure, in the name of the goddesses and gods. 99

ABOVE: *Salt and water (representing the elements of earth and water) are consecrated and mixed. The mixture is then used to consecrate the members of the coven and the circle.*

RIGHT: *A priest sweeps the circle using long, slow, and steady strokes. This is a symbolic action designed to clear the mind in preparation for ritual.*

LEFT: *The censer filled with burning incense (representing the elements of air and fire) is itself consecrated and then used to consecrate the people and the circle.*

★ Mix the two elements, saying:

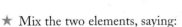

❝ *Earth and Water, sustaining and bonding, combine and balance your powers in our hearts in the most sacred names of Hermes, Aphrodite, and the Unconquered Sun.* ❞

★ Consecrate the members of the coven and then the temple.

★ Take up the censer with the incense, saying:

❝ *Air and Fire, inspiring and burning, combine and balance your power in our hearts in the most sacred names of Hermes, Aphrodite, and the Unconquered Sun.* ❞

★ Consecrate the members of the coven and then the temple with the smoke.

★ Draw the circle with the sword, saying:

❝ *This is a space between the worlds, here we will walk and speak with our goddesses and gods, a place of harmony, love, and peace, where ill will—our own and that of others—is unwelcome and will be turned aside in the most sacred names of Hermes, Aphrodite, and the Unconquered Sun.* ❞

★ Take the candle around the circle, saying:

❝ *In the most sacred names of Hermes, Aphrodite, and the Unconquered Sun, this space between the worlds is filled with light.* ❞

To complete the circle, you need to salute the elements. The ritual for this is outlined on pages 76–77 in *Saluting the Elements*.

LEFT: *The sword is used by the priestess to draw the circle. This creates sacred space within the temple in which rituals can take place.*

RIGHT: *A priestess hands a burning candle to a priest who takes it around the circle imagining the temple to be filled with pure white light.*

NOTES

Once you have set up a circle, do not breach it lightly (*see Cutting a Doorway, page 57.*)

Salt and water consecrated in the opening ritual may be used later in healing.

Goddess and god names have been inserted in this ritual for ease of reading. Feel free to substitute names of your own.

Saluting the Elements

To complete a circle that you are opening you need to greet the gods and goddesses at all four cardinal points. This is called saluting the elements. You may choose to visualize each element as a king, an element of nature, or as nature spirits.

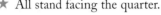

★ All stand facing the quarter.
★ The person saluting the element draws an invoking pentagram in the appropriate color, visualizes the element, and says "Hail and welcome" only when he or she feels that the quarter has responded.
★ All echo the "Hail and welcome."

RITUAL 1

East (blue): 66*Brothers and Sisters of the Eastern Quarter, Children of Air, Inspire our thinking, and share in our rite. Hail and welcome.*99

All: 66*Hail and welcome.*99

South (red/yellow):
66*Brothers and Sisters of the Southern Quarter, Children of Fire,*
*Brighten our vision, and share in our rite. Hail and welcome.*99

All: 66*Hail and welcome.*99

West (green):
66*Brothers and Sisters of the Western Quarter, Children of Water,*
*Unlock our feelings, and share in our rite. Hail and welcome.*99

All: 66*Hail and welcome.*99

North (yellow/brown):
66*Brothers and Sisters of the Northern Quarter, Children of Earth, enrich our work, and share in our rite. Hail and welcome.*99

All: 66*Hail and welcome.*99

ABOVE: *A priest stands facing the quarter and draws a pentagram of the appropriate color with his athame and visualizes the element as he calls it up, before saying "Hail and Welcome."*

1, 6

3

5

n

e

s

1, 6

4

2

ABOVE: *Some Wiccans choose to call upon the elemental kings: Eurius in the east, Notus in the south, Zephyrus in the west and Boreas in the north. These are the Greek names for the four winds.*

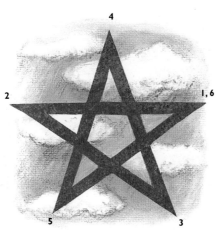

4

2

1, 6

5

3

LEFT: *The democratic option is to call on the elements at each quarter as brothers and sisters. Visualize nature spirits at play in air, fire, water, and earth.*

RITUAL 2

East: ❝*Eurius, Lord of Air and Guardian of the Watchtower of the East, we do summon, stir, and call you up to guard our circle and join in our rite. Blessed be thee.*❞

All: ❝*Blessed be thee.*❞

South: ❝*Notus, Lord of Fire and Guardian of the Watchtower of the South, we do summon, stir, and call you up to guard our circle and join in our rite. Blessed be thee.*❞

All: ❝*Blessed be thee.*❞

West: ❝*Zephyrus, Lord of Water and Guardian of the Watchtower of the West, we do summon, stir, and call you up to guard our circle and join in our rite. Blessed be thee.*❞

All: ❝*Blessed be thee.*❞

North: ❝*Boreas, Lord of Earth and Guardian of the Watchtower of the North, we do summon, stir, and call you up to guard our circle and join in our rite. Blessed be thee.*❞

All: ❝*Blessed be thee.*❞

Raising Energy

Raising energy can be done in a variety of ways: singing, chanting, dancing, and visualization (guided or otherwise). Here are some suggestions for raising energy, starting with a popular traditional song.

JOHN BARLEYCORN

1 There were three men from
    Oxford came
To plow for wheat and rye
And they made a vow, a solemn vow —
John Barleycorn must die.

2 They laid him in three furrows deep,
Laid clods upon his head,
  Then these three men made a
    solemn vow
    John Barleycorn was dead.

3 And there he lay for some
    long time
    'Til the rains from the skies
      did fall,
      Then Barleycorn popped up
his head
And did surprise them all.

4 He grew up tall in the midsummer
    time
When the weather was pleasant and
    warm
And then he grew a furry beard
To prove he was a man.

5 Then they hired men with sickles
To cut him off at the knee
And how they used poor
    Barleycorn
They used him barbarously.

6 They hired men with crabtree
    sticks
To cut him skin from bone
And the miller he served him worse
than that
For he ground him between two
    stones.

7 Then they pushed him into a
    tub so strong
And kept him in the barn
And there they made a mash of him
Thinking it would do no harm.

8 They worked their will on John
    Barleycorn
But he lived to tell the tale
For they pour him out of an old
    brown jug
And they call him homebrewed ale.

ABOVE: *The folk song* John Barleycorn *celebrates the life cycle of the barley. Under the surface humor lie intimations of ancient sacrificial traditions. Barleycorn must die to be reborn as homebrewed ale.*

ROOTS AND BRANCHES

This is a guided visualization exercise that helps to raise energy for the cone of power. It does not matter whether you are in a ground floor room or not.

★ All coven members stand comfortably.
★ They close their eyes.
★ The leader says:

66 Your feet sink into the ground, becoming roots growing deep into our Mother the Earth. Her energies are all around, rising up like sap through your feet and legs; filling your body. Feel them in every cell. You are at one with Her.

You are a great strong tree. Stand tall with arms upstretched. These are your branches reaching up to our Father the Sky. Your leaves drink in the power of the Sun. The energies course down your arms and into the center of your being. Earth and sky energies mix. Feel the life-giving energy swirling throughout your body. More energy is taken in with every breath. Fill the circle with this energy. Continue to draw it in and to send it out. You are at one with all that is. The life that pulses through nature, pulses through you. 99

MANTRAS

★ Make a simple chant using the names of the goddess and god you are going to invoke.
★ Rearrange them until the syllables flow rhythmically. It only needs to be a simple mantralike chant. One example is:

66 Re, He–ca–te." Another is "Ven–us, Mer–cur–ius, Sol In–vic–tus. 99

★ If you have drums, rattles, tambourines, or other percussion instruments, use them to emphasize the beat.
★ Dance around in a circle or weave in and out.
★ If unable to dance, sit and sway with your eyes closed. Feel the chant resonate within you.

LEFT: *Raise energy with chants and mark the beat with percussion instruments. Simple chants can be made using the names of the goddess and god you will be invoking.*

CASTING SPELLS

This is a traditional spell, known as *The Mill*, and is used to raise and send energy for any purpose.

Dance around the cauldron, focusing on your magical intent and chant the following rhyme:

66 Air breathe and air blow
Make the mill of magic grow

Fire flame and fire burn
Make the mill of magic turn

Work the will for which we pray
Eo deo ha hay yay

Water heat and water boil
Make the mill of magic toil

(Repeat this chorus after each of the four verses.)

Earth without and earth within
Make the mill of magic spin. 99

Invocations and Charges

To call a goddess or god into a person in the circle, we use an invocation. *The words of the deity that are then spoken through that person are known as the* charge. *The invocation and the charge can be combined to make an* evocation, *that is, words that are used to call the deity into the circle, but not into a person inside the circle. Below are examples of evocations for Hermes and Aphrodite, but you are encouraged to combine the other invocations and charges as you wish— and, of course, to write your own.*

BELOW: *Hermes is the messenger of the Greek gods. He is a rogue and a charmer. He is often shown as a handsome young man wearing a winged or horned cap.*

A WORD OF WARNING

Goddesses and gods can be awkward houseguests. Do not call on one that you would not be happy to have in your home. Even if you ask them to leave, they may still hang around.

They and the four elements have different rules from us. Fire elementals love fire and have been known to help speed up the cooking with skillet fires. Pan is definitely not a cuddly figure. One of the effects of having Pan around is *PANic* (or *PANdemonium*).

You need to be careful how you speak to deities and elementals; they dislike being bossed around as much as you do.

HERMES

Hermes is the Greek God of Communication, Magic, Medicine, Merchants, Thieves, and Liars.

Hermes Invocation

❝ *Hermes, Master of Magic, shepherd of dreams, creator of form, child of the mountains, shower of ways, come to this your priest who loves you. Speak to us.* ❞

Hermes Charge

❝ *I am the cairn beside the road,
The sure guide to the mysteries,
Touched by my wand your wildest dreams
Take on the shapes of beasts and men.
Accept my rule, let your mind be filled
With the undying splendor of the sun.* ❞

Hermes Evocation

❝ *Hermes, Master of Magic, shepherd of dreams, creator of form, child of the mountains, shower of ways, you who are the cairn by the roadside, the sure guide to the mysteries. Touched by your rod, our wildest dreams take on the shapes of beast and men. You are my lord. Let my mind be filled with the undying splendor of the sun.* ❞

APHRODITE

Aphrodite is the Greek Goddess of Love (Roman name: Venus). She is often accompanied by her infant son Eros, God of Love.

Aphrodite Invocation

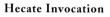 *Aphrodite, star of the sea, maker of poets, breaker of hearts, queen of love and mistress of beauty, come to this your priestess who loves you. Speak to us.*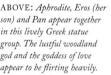

Aphrodite Charge

*I am the wedding of sea and shore,
The break of the wave, the leap of the foam.
Innocent laughter follows me.
Wherever I am, a garden grows.
Mine are the mysteries of pleasure and love.
Drink of the cup of my victory.*

Aphrodite Evocation

Aphrodite, star of the sea, maker of poets, breaker of hearts, queen of love and mistress of beauty. You are the wedding of sea and shore, the break of the wave, the leap of the foam, innocent laughter follows you. Wherever you are, a garden grows. Yours are the mysteries of pleasure and love. I drink of the cup of your victory.

★ Drink to her from the chalice.

HECATE

Hecate is the Greek Triple Goddess, Goddess of the Underworld and of Witches. She is associated with crossroads.

ABOVE: *Aphrodite, Eros (her son) and Pan appear together in this lively Greek statue group. The lustful woodland god and the goddess of love appear to be flirting heavily.*

Hecate Invocation

Great Mother, queen of all witcheries, wisdom, dragon-guarded spring, shining moon, cave of voices, bitter sea; of thy great love, come to us and speak to us through thy priestess and servant.

Hecate Charge

*Where roads divide, at river crossings,
Among the tombs, in your secret heart,
I lie in wait with my troublesome questions.
Face me and you face your fear.
Accept my challenge and enter the dark.
Only through me will you find the new.*

PAN

Pan is the Greek God of the Wild Wood. He is portrayed with cloven hooves, shaggy thighs, horns, and panpipes.

Pan Invocation

O my Lord, companion, brother, fiery sun, undaunted heart, maker of music, pathfinder, goat-footed god, in good fellowship come to us and speak to us through thy priest and servant.

LEFT: *Aphrodite, Goddess of Love, says: "I am the wedding of sea and shore, the break of the wave, the leap of the foam. Innocent laughter follows me."*

ABOVE: *Pan is shown as master of the beasts in this 16th-century fresco by Giovanni Falconetto. In the background the nymph Europa is carried off by Zeus disguised as a bull.*

Pan Charge

❝*I am the piper at the gates of dawn. My sweet music teases you on From lifetime to lifetime. I am desire And hope and courage. Listen to me Above the hubbub, below the silence. I am the voice of your innermost heart.*❞

SUMMER GOD

Some Wiccans prefer their gods to be nameless. The Summer God is a personification of the spirit of summer and should be visualized as a vigorous young man.

Summer God Invocation

❝*O Lord of the May, come to us, giver of the seed of life, come to us. Bringer of the noontime dreams, return to those who seek thy love. Come to the body of thy priest and servant, O Lord of the summer dance, come.*❞

RIGHT: *The Summer God is a personification of the spirit of summer. He says: "I am desire and youth and love and the endlessness of the summer sky."*

Summer God Charge

❝*I am the god your mothers worshiped. I am the dance on the village green. I am the night of stars and branches. I am a tall stone bedded in earth, my shadow wheeling across the field; around my head the singing birds, around my feet the meadow grasses. I am the Bright and Beautiful One. I am desire and youth and love and the endlessness of the summer sky.*❞

YULETIDE GODDESS

The Yuletide Goddess is a composite of the Great Mother Goddesses who give birth to the Divine Child at the Winter Solstice.

Yuletide Goddess Invocation

❝*Goddess I call you, Lady of Lights, whose name is Isis, Freya, Mary, Brighid, Venus, giver of gifts and mother of children, star crowned in your winter furs, bless us now as the year turns.*❞

Yuletide
Goddess Charge

❝I am the mother of gods and men. I bring them into the light and then into the dark. Within my womb the generations wait to bring the golden age to the Earth again. I am wisdom and I am love, as deep and wide as the starry skies. Be ever blessed in knowing me.❞

HERNE

Herne is the British Stag God, leader of the Wild Hunt. He is associated with Windsor Great Park in England.

Herne Invocation

❝Herne, Herne, Mighty Lord of hill and wood, come to us O horned one, lover, jester, oaken king, mighty huntsman, and hunted stag. Herne, Herne, come to my call, Herne, Herne, come to my call, Herne, Herne, come to my call.❞

Herne Charge

❝I ride the wind upon Albion's hills, I carry the sun between my antlers, I am Herne of the wizard oak, I am Herne of the flighted arrow, Terror to tyrants, hope to the poor, Outlaw, huntsman, demon lover, I break the dead from their graves. The chains That I have shattered hang from my wrists.❞

HERTHA

Hertha is the Germanic Earth Goddess.

Hertha Invocation

❝I call on you, our Mother the Earth, whom we have so often wronged and slighted. Turn your face kindly on us, your children. Do not dismiss us but strengthen us. O most bountiful, o most beautiful, speak to us now through your priestess who loves you.❞

Hertha Charge

❝I come to you sorrowful and forsaken. I am the warm-hearted mother who gives birth to all things. Upon my body all life lives and feeds; without me all things cease to exist. All life is born of my love. Yet some do not love me. Beware my brokenhearted wrath, lest I turn my body from you. Yet I gain strength from you, the children who love me and I thank you for the hope you bring.❞

LEFT: *Wiccans decorate their temples at Yule. The priestess invoked as the Yuletide Goddess might well wear a chaplet or crown of winter evergreens and berries.*

BELOW: *Herne the hunter, the British Stag God, has been seen in Windsor Great Park in England. He has antlers on his brows and leads a troop of specters in the Wild Hunt.*

Blessing Cakes and Wine

The blessing of cakes and wine is a symbolic form of the Great Rite and takes place at every esbat or sabbat. Following the blessing is a love feast or family meal. In most cultures the sharing of food and drink is a central sacrament that binds the participants together as brothers and sisters. For many there is no greater crime than to harm a person with whom you have "broken bread."

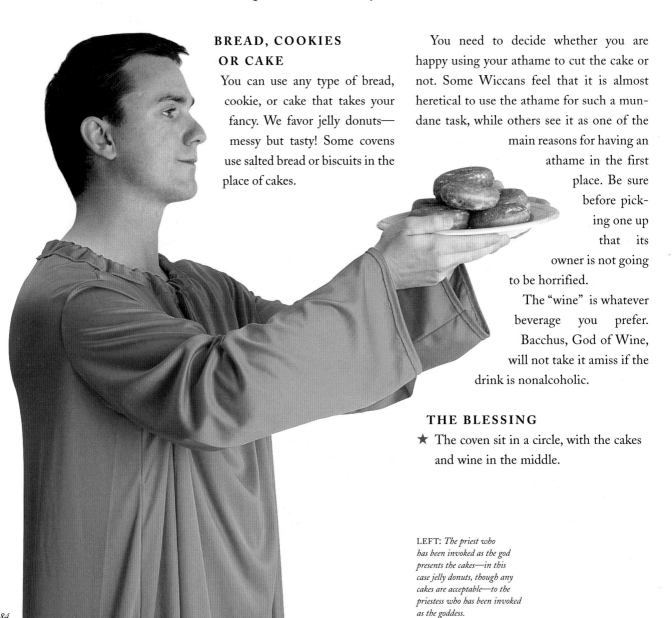

BREAD, COOKIES OR CAKE

You can use any type of bread, cookie, or cake that takes your fancy. We favor jelly donuts—messy but tasty! Some covens use salted bread or biscuits in the place of cakes.

You need to decide whether you are happy using your athame to cut the cake or not. Some Wiccans feel that it is almost heretical to use the athame for such a mundane task, while others see it as one of the main reasons for having an athame in the first place. Be sure before picking one up that its owner is not going to be horrified.

The "wine" is whatever beverage you prefer. Bacchus, God of Wine, will not take it amiss if the drink is nonalcoholic.

THE BLESSING

★ The coven sit in a circle, with the cakes and wine in the middle.

LEFT: *The priest who has been invoked as the god presents the cakes—in this case jelly donuts, though any cakes are acceptable—to the priestess who has been invoked as the goddess.*

* The priest and priestess who have been invoked sit with them, facing one another.
* The priest holds up the plate of cakes and says:

66 *All things come from goddess and god, and all things return to them.* 99

* The priestess draws an earth-invoking pentagram over the cakes with her athame (*see* pages 76–77), touching each one, and says:

66 *May the blessings of Herne and Aradia be on this food.* 99

* She breaks off a morsel of cake and gives it to the priest.
* She eats a morsel herself.
* The plate is returned to the center of the circle, and everyone helps themselves.
* The priest holds up the full chalice.
* The priestess plunges her athame into it and says:

66 *May the blessing of Herne and Aradia be on this drink.* 99

* She gives the priest a sip and has a sip herself.
* The chalice is passed around the circle, deosil.
* Everyone toasts a goddess and a god.

A small amount of both cakes and wine are kept back to be used as a libation.

CONSECRATION

New items of temple paraphernalia are consecrated at this point. This is done by passing them three times through each of the elements.

* First pass the item through the smoke from the censer three times.
* Then pass it through the flame of the candle at south three times.
* Sprinkle it with water.
* Rub it with salt or dry soil.
* Finally, a priest and priestess embrace (she stands with her toes on his feet, making a circle), holding the object securely between their chests.

It is now ready for use. Items for use in magic may be consecrated at any time using this technique.

When an item has been used and is no longer needed it should be deconsecrated or cleansed. This is done by placing it on a window ledge, where it will be bathed in sunlight and moonlight, for one full cycle of the moon.

Following cakes and wine is the time for dancing, singing, and games.

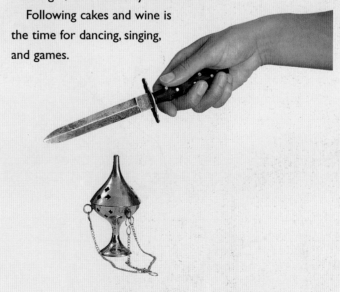

Closing a Circle

When all the work has been done, and the cakes and wine have been blessed, it is time to close the circle. There are no strict rules for this (see page 70), but here are some suggested rituals for dissipating the energies raised and bringing the coven members back down to earth.

DISPERSING ENERGIES

When god and goddess have been *invoked* into a priest and priestess, the process of earthing followed by blessing cakes and wine is usually sufficient to disperse the energies.

When god and goddess have been *evoked*, you will need to make a conscious effort to disperse the energy. Do this by sending them on their way with this farewell:

RIGHT: *When the god and goddess have been invoked a simple embrace will disperse their energy. Where they have been evoked it is best to bid them a verbal farewell.*

66(Names) *I thank you for your help and guidance. I ask for your blessing as you now depart to your fair and lovely realm. Hail and farewell.* 99

★ Then dismiss the elements.

DISMISSING THE ELEMENTS

The following blessing prayer, which invokes Dryghten the Great Spirit, may be said before the elements are dismissed.

66*In the name of Dryghten the Ancient Providence which was from the beginning and is for eternity, both male and female, the original source of all things; all knowing, all pervading, all powerful, changeless, and eternal; in the name of Our Lady of the Moon and the Lord of Death and Resurrection; in the names of the Mighty Ones of the four quarters, the Kings of the Elements, we do say, blessed be this place and this time and they who are with us. Blessed be.* 99

You may then wish to carry out one of the following rituals. Draw the elemental pentagram in reverse at each quarter as you say the words. Imagine that you are rubbing it out or else drawing the energy back into your athame.

Ritual 1

East (blue): 66*Brothers and Sisters of the Eastern Quarter, Children of Air, we thank you for your presence and your guidance. Hail and farewell.* 99

All: 66 *Hail and farewell.* 99

South (red/yellow): 66 *Brothers and Sisters of the Southern Quarter, Children of Fire, we thank you for your presence and your guidance. Hail and farewell.* 99

All: 66 *Hail and farewell.* 99

West (green): 66 *Brothers and Sisters of the Western Quarter, Children of Water, we thank you for your presence and your guidance. Hail and farewell.* 99

All: 66 *Hail and farewell.* 99

North (yellow/brown):
66 *Brothers and Sisters of the Northern Quarter, Children of Earth, we thank you for your presence and your guidance. Hail and farewell.* 99

All: 66 *Hail and farewell.* 99

Ritual 2
East: 66 *Eurius, Lord of Air and Guardian of the Watchtower of the East, farewell. Thank you for your help and guidance. Blessed be thee.* 99

All: 66 *Blessed be thee.* 99

South: 66 *Notus, Lord of Fire and Guardian of the Watchtower of the South, farewell. Thank you for your help and guidance. Blessed be thee.* 99

All: 66 *Blessed be thee.* 99

West: 66 *Zephyrus, Lord of Water and Guardian of the Watchtower of the West, farewell. Thank you for your help and guidance. Blessed be thee.* 99

All: 66 *Blessed be thee.* 99

North: 66 *Boreas, Lord of Earth and Guardian of the Watchtower of the North, farewell. Thank you for your help and guidance. Blessed be thee.* 99

All: 66 *Blessed be thee.* 99

MERRY MEET
★ Before the coven members leave the temple the high priestess leads the people in saying:

66 *Merry meet, merry part, and merry meet again.* 99

★ Everyone hugs and kisses everyone else.
★ The candles are then extinguished using a snuffer. Do not blow candles out—it is considered to be bad manners.
★ A priest and priestess are delegated to libate.
★ They take portions of food and drink outside and scatter them on the ground.

ABOVE: *At the end of a ritual candles should be snuffed or pinched out with the fingers. It is bad manners —and some would say unlucky —to blow them out.*

BELOW: *The elemental pentagram should be drawn in reverse at each quarter. Imagine that you are rubbing it out or drawing the energy back into your athame.*

Imbolc Ritual

Imbolc, a Celtic festival, is celebrated on February 1–2 as the spring is about to return. This time of the strengthening light and regrowth is a time for getting rid of personal, spiritual, and psychological baggage.

PREPARATION

★ Before the ritual spring-clean and tidy the temple.

★ Put the greenery from Yule, corn from Lammas, and any other flammable decorations to one side (these will be burned later).

★ Make the temple dark except for one candle lit in the cauldron, which is in the center of the room.

★ Everyone is given two pieces of paper. On one they write something they wish to give away, eg, intolerance; on the other they write something they wish to gain.

★ Open the circle, using the Imbolc opening invocation below.

★ Salute the elements.

RIGHT: *Following the casting of the circle, and in anticipation of Juno Februata's charge, three priestesses stand holding white candles which Juno Februata will light from hers.*

OPENING INVOCATION

❝ The wheel turns and we are at Imbolc, a time when we feel bowed down by the dark. Yet there are signs of new life all around us. The Earth shows us the first flowers of spring. The night withdraws and the days lengthen. Our homes appear dusty and dull, but the fire is burning strong in the sacred hearth of the goddess. Let us take heart and clean away the grime of winter. ❞

ENERGY-RAISING CHANT

❝ Juno called Februata, Juno of Fevers,
Flu and the common cold, agues and sneezes,
May the love sickness, the fever of rutting,
Drive out the grouchy ill-ease of the shut-in.
See the bright crocus, like Candlemas candles,
Promise us light summer dresses and sandals. ❞

★ Move the cauldron to one side.

★ The priestess to be invoked holds an unlit yellow candle as she stands in god position.

★ All others hold unlit white candles.

JUNO FEBRUATA CHARGE

❝I am Juno Februata. Now is the time when I am strongest. I turn my eyes toward you and the light blossoms. I take away the darkness. I put new life in the fields; I brighten your lives with spring flowers. You called to me and I have answered. I give you my blessing.❞

★ Juno lights her candle from the one in the cauldron.

★ She moves around, lighting the candles held by the coven. (*If you have evoked the goddess, light your own candle from the cauldron.*)

★ All move around the temple lighting candles from their own.

★ The goddess is earthed by her invoker.

★ Everyone sits around the cauldron.

★ They burn the "giving back" papers one at a time, saying:

❝Juno Februata, I ask for your help to rid myself of (say what is written on the paper).❞

★ When these have all been burned, everyone takes up the other piece of paper and burns it, saying:

❝Great Mother, help me to gain (name it) so I may serve you better.❞

★ Cakes and wine.

★ Close the circle.

★ Go outside and burn the old decorations that were put aside earlier.

Note: This is a time for having as many candles as possible in the temple. You will need empty candlesticks to put the held candles in once they are lit.

JUNO FEBRUATA INVOCATION

❝Juno, Great Mother, light that enlightens every woman, mistress of mirth and love, hostess and provider of the feast, turn your dark eyes toward us now, encourage us, and speak to us through this your priestess who loves you.❞

LEFT: *Juno Februata lights her yellow candle from the one in the cauldron before moving around to light the candles of the attendant priests and priestesses.*

ABOVE: *Juno is queen of the Roman Gods and one of the three patrons of the city of Rome. In art she is generally portrayed as a handsome, mature woman.*

Spring Equinox Ritual

The spring equinox is celebrated on March 21–22. Day and night are now equal, and from here on days will lengthen. It is a time of fertility and new life.

PREPARATION

★ Put potting soil in one large pot and enough small pots for each person to plant seeds in. These will be taken home after the ritual.

★ Put the pots and some seeds onto an altar.

★ The person saying the opening invocation holds a black candle in their left hand and a white candle in the right.

★ When lit, these candles should be put either side of the altar (black to the left and white to the right).

★ Cast the circle using the equinox opening invocation below.

★ Salute the elements.

BELOW: *The altar is set with a black and a white candle symbolizing that day and night are equal. Pots, potting soil, and seeds are set ready for a ritual planting.*

OPENING INVOCATION

❝*Night and day are equal. The sun and moon are in perfect balance. The reign of darkness is over.*❞

★ Light the black and then the white candle from the altar candle.

❝*The left and the right, the dark and the light.*❞

ENERGY-RAISING CHANT

❝*Come, come to the heartbeat's drum.*❞

★ Repeat at least nine times.

God is invoked in the north quarter; goddess is invoked in the south quarter.

DIONYSUS INVOCATION

❝*God of the springtide, mighty Dionysus, twiceborn, Lord of life and lust, of freedom and ecstasy, leader of the dance, come, descend upon the body of thy servant and priest.*❞

DIONYSUS CHARGE

❝*I am Dionysus, the Lord of rapture, bestower of riches, destroyer of men. I govern the tides that flow through nature. I am the blood and the sap and the sperm.*❞

ABOVE: *The god uses his athame to bless the seeds that he has planted in a bowl of earth placed on the goddess's abdomen, as she lies in the pentacle position.*

★ God catches goddess.

★ She drinks from the chalice and passes the cup to the priest.

★ God and goddess embrace.

★ The symbolic Great Rite is enacted; priests and priestesses give them the bowl of earth, seeds, and athame. The bowl of earth is placed on the goddess's abdomen, as she lies in pentacle position.

★ The god plants the seeds in the bowl of earth and consecrates them with the athame, saying:

66 *I sow the seeds that bring forth new life.* 99

★ He then says:

66 *I make fruitful that which has borne no fruit. I make as one the male and the female.* 99

★ He plunges the athame into the earth.

66 *The god and the goddess, the two and the one.* 99

★ The bowl in which the seeds have been planted, any remaining seeds, and the athame are handed to the priest and priestess.

★ The god helps the goddess to rise.

★ The goddess says:

66 *Let us sow the seeds of life that shall bring forth new hope, new deeds, and even as these seeds shoot forth and grow green, so may new life be manifest within us.* 99

★ Everyone plants seeds in small pots.

★ The invokers earth the god and goddess.

★ Cakes and wine and close the circle.

APHRODITE INVOCATION

66 *I invoke and call upon thee, Aphrodite, most beautiful flower-faced maiden of spring, for flowers lead to fruit as loving leads to conception. By life and love do I ask thee to descend upon the body of thy servant and priestess.* 99

APHRODITE CHARGE

66 *I am Aphrodite, born of the foaming seas, devouring spider, and queen bee. My smile brings wild desire, inspiring man to lunacy, love, and poetry. I am always there at the edge of your vision.* 99

★ Maiden passes full chalice to god.

★ Aphrodite touches the god's face and says:

66 *Follow me and I will dance with you. My dance is unknown and yet must be perfect. Will you dance with me and risk my disappointment?* 99

★ God replies:

66 *Will you drink of my wine?* 99

★ Goddess moves away without drinking.

★ God dances after her.

Beltane Ritual

Beltane is celebrated from April 30 to May 1 as a time when nature is fresh and the herds are being driven to the summer pasturelands. It is a time for planning new projects, a time for new, untried activities.

PREPARATION

★ Deck the temple with seasonal greenery.

★ Make floral crowns for the women and crowns of greenery for the men.

★ Each coven member brings a small symbol of their work (for example, a teacher could bring an exercise book).

★ Cast the circle, using the Beltane opening invocation below.

★ Salute the elements.

RIGHT: *In this ancient bronze statuette from Iceland, the Norse god Thor is shown wearing a steel helmet with his mighty hammer Miolnir clasped between his knees.*

OPENING INVOCATION

66 The wheel turns and we come to Beltane with its promise of summer to come. The corn in the fields stretches toward the sky. Thor chases away the storms from the east so that Sif can watch her grasslands grow. This is the season for marriages. We ask the gods to bless us in work and play. 99

ENERGY RAISING

66 Oh, do not tell the priest our plight
Or he would call it a sin;
But—we have been out in the woods all night,
A-conjuring summer in!
And we bring you news by word of mouth—
Good news for cattle and corn—
Now is the sun come up from the south,
With oak, and ash, and thorn! 99

ABOVE: *Sif crowns the women with floral crowns and the men with crowns of greenery, saying "Work and play go hand in hand . . . Enjoy this holy day."*

★ *The goddess and god are invoked side by side with their backs to the altar.*

THOR INVOCATION

66 Red-bearded Thor, god of the Northlands, Lord of good weather, champion of the people, beloved husband of Sif, come to us; speak to us through this your priest who loves you. 99

SIF INVOCATION

66 Sif of the golden hair, Lady of the northern grasslands and wheatfields, bearer of the sickle, beloved wife of Thor, come to us; speak to us through this your priestess who loves you. 99

★ Sif crowns Thor with a kiss and says:
66 My grasslands feed the laborers. 99

★ Thor crowns Sif with a kiss and says:
66 My labor makes the homesteads strong. 99

* Members of the coven present their symbol of work to Thor.
* Thor places these symbols on the altar and says:

66 *May your work prosper. Whatever you do, you do for all. Enjoy this holy day.* 99

* Members of the coven kneel before Sif.
* Sif crowns them with a garland and says:

66 *Work and play go hand in hand. Receive this symbol of life and love. Enjoy this holy day.* 99

Sif: 66 *May the earth rejoice in the labor of its sons and daughters.* 99

Thor: 66 *May the rivers run clear and unpolluted.* 99

Sif: 66 *May the fields be full of golden grain.* 99

Thor: 66 *May the towns be full of light and plenty.* 99

Sif: 66 *May every homestead ring with laughter.* 99

Thor: 66 *May the roads be safe, and the land know peace.* 99

* The invokers earth the god and goddess with an embrace.
* Cakes and wine.
* Close the circle.
* Everyone collects their work item from the altar to take home.

ABOVE: *Thor receives a symbol of her work from a priestess and says: "May your work prosper. Whatever you do, you do for all. Enjoy this holy day."*

Midsummer Solstice Ritual

Midsummer solstice is celebrated on June 21–22. It is a time of perfection, the mystical marriage of heaven and earth. And yet it is also a time of curious sadness, because it marks the point at which the days will start to shorten again. When the sun is at its brightest, it casts the deepest shadows.

PREPARATION

★ A symbol of the sun—it might be a wheel or a large circular loaf—is placed on the altar.

★ Prepare a club (a baseball bat or suitably shaped piece of wood) and put it in the south where Hera can reach it.

★ Remove the black and white candles of the Spring Equinox festival.

★ Replace them with two yellow candles.

★ Prepare the cauldron, and put it in the south quarter until needed.

★ Cast the circle, using the midsummer opening invocation below.

★ Salute the elements.

OPENING INVOCATION

❝*As we celebrate the power of the sun at the time of the bonfire on the hill, we remember how Hercules, mortally wounded, built his pyre on the summit of Etna and, taken apart by the flames,* rose to be a god in heaven, and husband to Hebe, Goddess of Youth.❞

ENERGY RAISING

❝*The sun stands still in the height of heaven,
All things must pass away.*

*The days of summer stretch ahead,
All things must pass away.*

*Welcome the days of flowers and fruit,
All things must pass away.*

*Welcome the days of leisure and love,
All things must pass away.*

*Now is the wedding of earth and heaven,
All things must pass away.*❞

★ The cauldron is placed in front of Hera, who is invoked in the south quarter.

LEFT: *Two yellow candles replace the black and white ones that have stood on the altar since Spring Equinox. They flank a circular loaf, which symbolizes the sun at its strength.*

HERA INVOCATION

66 *Mighty Hera, all-seeing goddess, just and implacable, open foe and secret friend to Hercules. You who shape the heroic soul through adversity, come, descend, speak to us through this your priestess who loves you.* 99

HERA CHARGE (AND HERCULES INVOCATION)

66 *I am Hera, queen of the Gods. I am just, but never cruel; I take the hero and make him divine. Without my punishing help, he would not know the divine spark within. If I did not enslave him, he would never know freedom. I am the maker of Hercules.* 99

66 *Come, Hercules.* 99

★ Hercules moves to stand before her, with the cauldron on the floor between them.

66 *I set you the tests that affirm you as son of Zeus. Take this club, for you are the righter of wrongs, the madman who kills those he loves the most. Lecher. Glutton. And people's champion. Speak to us, mighty Hercules.* 99

★ Hercules takes the club from Hera.

HERCULES CHARGE

66 *I am he whose name means glory of Hera, the blunt instrument of divine will. I choose virtue and do right as I see it, defending the weak and the poor. I bring terror to tyrants and men without honor. In my death I bear humanity up to heaven. I live in you and make you divine.* 99

★ Hercules lights a fire, or a candle, in the cauldron, and says:

66 *To reach perfection of desire
The lover passes through the fire
And casting mortal dress aside,
Rises in smoke to meet the bride.* 99

★ The god and goddess are then earthed by their invokers with an embrace.
★ All meditate around the cauldron.
★ Cakes and wine.
★ Close the circle.

ABOVE: *Hercules takes the club from Hera and says: "I am he whose name means glory of Hera, the blunt instrument of divine will."*

Lammas Ritual

Lammas, celebrated from July 31 to August 1 , is the time of the grain harvest. It is a time of growth and change, and a time for introspection. Its theme is transformation through suffering and sacrifice.

PREPARATION

★ Decorate the temple with corn, barley, and other stalks of grain and, if possible, corn dollies.

★ A small sheaf of corn or other grain is put on the altar for the Corn God to hold.

★ Leave the yellow midsummer candles in place.

★ Cast the circle, using the Lammas opening invocation below.

★ Salute the elements.

OPENING INVOCATION

66 *The wheel turns and we celebrate the time of harvest, thanking god and goddess for their gifts. Though most of us are well removed from the physical labor of sowing and reaping, we reaffirm our dependency on the Earth. She is our Mother and all living things are her children and are bound together in the great chain of being.* 99

ENERGY RAISING

★ Sing or chant all or part of John Barleycorn (*see page 78*) or do Roots and Branches (*see page 79*).

★ The priest to be invoked as the Corn God stands with his back to the altar holding a sheaf of corn.

★ Behind him on the altar place a loaf of bread and a glass of beer.

RIGHT: *At Lammas the temple is decorated with stalks of grain in celebration of the harvest. A corn dollie stands on the altar alongside plaits and sheaves of grain.*

CORN GOD INVOCATION

" *Spirit of the corn, golden in the fields, you bow and sway to the music of the wind. We come to cut you down. Your time of metamorphosis is here. By the standing sheaf I call you. By the grain of wheat I call you. By the risen loaf I call you. Come to us, speak to us through this your priest who loves you.* "

CORN GOD CHARGE

" *I will be reaped that you may eat. I will be broken to make your bread. My blood will flow in beer and wine. I shall become what I want to be, the sustenance of the folk. In you I shall achieve repose and wisdom.* "

★ The Corn God drops the corn and steps aside into northwest, revealing the loaf and glass on the altar.

★ His invoker earths him with an embrace.

LAMMAS REPLACEMENT FOR CAKES AND WINE

★ A priestess takes some bread and presents it to the people, saying:

" *Mother, Father, bless this bread, your gift, and our labor. As we eat may we remember that we are links in the chain of being.* "

★ A priest takes the beer and presents it to the people, saying:

" *Mother, Father, bless this ale, your gift, and our labor. As we drink may we remember that we are one with all that lives.* "

★ Pass bread and beer around the circle, deosil.

★ Make toasts to the god and goddess.

★ Close the circle.

★ Turn the corn used by the god into an altar decoration, for burning at Imbolc.

BELOW: *A priest takes the beer and presents it to the people, saying: "Mother, Father, bless this ale, your gift and our labor ... we are one with all that lives."*

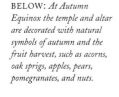

Autumn Equinox Ritual

The autumn equinox is celebrated on September 21–22. At this point day and night are equal and the nights begin to get longer. It is a time for wistful reflection on the transience of life.

PREPARATION

★ Deck the temple with natural symbols of autumn, such as acorns, oak sprigs, fruit, and nuts.

★ Remove the yellow candles of Lammas and put a white candle in the northwest and a black candle in the northeast.

★ Cast the circle, using the equinox opening invocation below.

★ Salute the elements.

OPENING INVOCATION

❝Day and night are equal.❞

★ Light the candles.

❝The darkness grows apace and we turn inward. The fallen seeds rest in the Earth. Kore takes leave of her mother Demeter and returns to the Underworld, where she becomes Persephone and reigns as queen among the dead. 'If winter comes, can spring be far behind?'❞

ENERGY RAISING

❝Hear the thunder of the wheels
As the tyrant comes who steals
Kore from the world of men.
Dead leaves tumble from the trees.
It will snow and it will freeze
Ere the goddess comes again.❞

PERSEPHONE INVOCATION

❝Persephone, flower-faced maiden of spring, innocent Kore, innocent loving daughter of Demeter, you who have gladdened the spring and summer fields, come to us; speak to us through this your priestess who loves you.❞

BELOW: At Autumn Equinox the temple and altar are decorated with natural symbols of autumn and the fruit harvest, such as acorns, oak sprigs, apples, pears, pomegranates, and nuts.

RIGHT: In Greek mythology Hades rules an underworld where the wicked suffer punishment and the good reside in the blissful Elysian Fields. Persephone rules at his side for half the year.

HADES INVOCATION

66 *Hades, Lord of the Underworld, collector of souls, husband of our beloved Persephone, come to us; speak to us through this your priest who loves you.* 99

★ The god and goddess turn to face one another.
★ Hades says:

66 *Leave the dances, my love; it is time*
To return to our kingdom under the Earth.
The white-faced ghosts are looking for you.
The winds give tongue. The dead leaves fall. 99

★ Persephone replies:

66 *I toss the seed from my skirts. Behind me*
The meadows die that will bloom in spring.
I change my dance for a Sarabande.
And go where smoky torches burn
And dead men watch my every step
In hope of a kindly word from me. 99

★ Hades turns to the people gathered and says:

66 *Eat the dust of my wheels. You people*
Will follow us soon. 99

★ Persephone turns to the people, radiates energy, and says:

66 *My husband's harsh.*
I bring the two worlds under one scepter
Though I head for the dark I am still
The woman I was, your friend and neighbor.
Wait till the seed I scattered has grown
To flowers and grass
And you'll see me again.
And we shall have fine times out in the sun. 99

★ Invokers earth the god and goddess with an embrace.
★ Cakes and wine.
★ Close the circle.

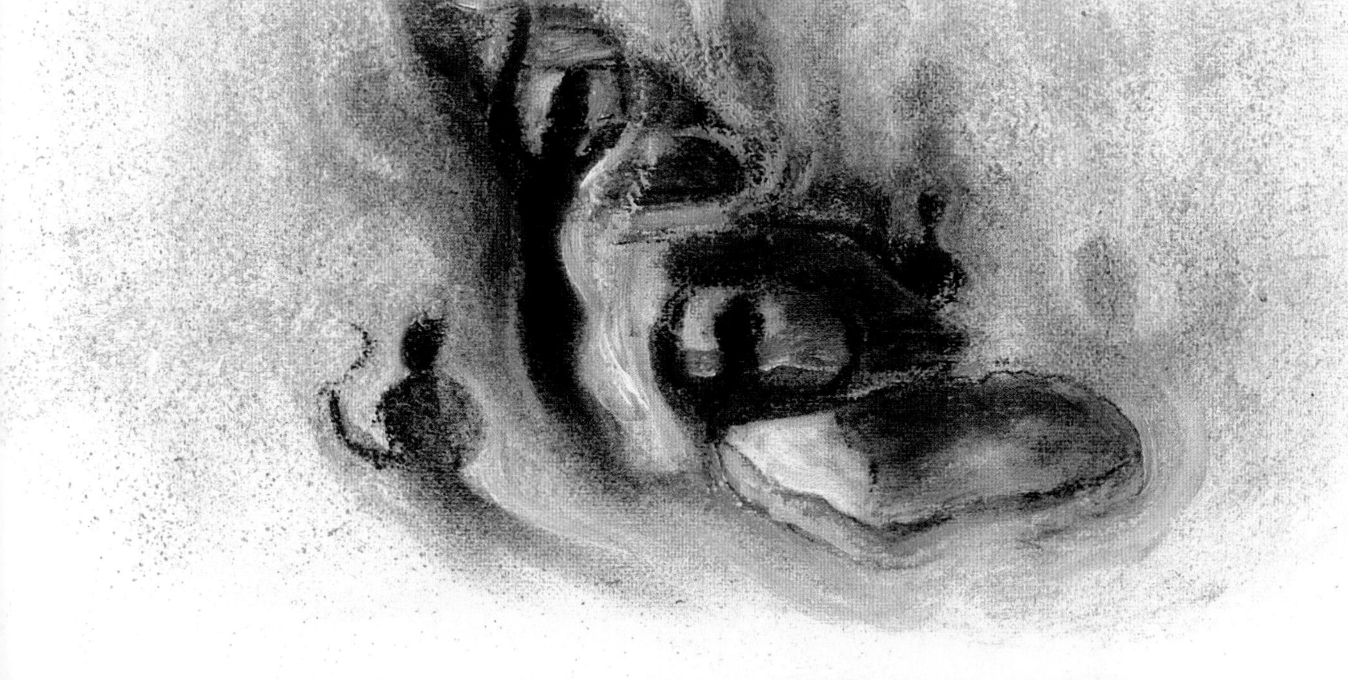

Samhain Ritual

Samhain, celebrated from October 31 to November 1, was originally established to keep people's spirits up during the winter months. It was a time when kings and warlords gathered their subjects for sports and feasting. Herds were culled to make winter fodder go further and festivities with lights and fires were held.

PREPARATION

★ Remove all flowers and decorations from the temple.

★ Add a second black candle to the black and white candles of autumn equinox.

★ Cast the circle, using the Samhain opening invocation below.

★ Salute the quarters.

OPENING INVOCATION

❝ *The light grows weaker. The ground is dank beneath our feet. The veil between the worlds is thin. We stand before the gates of Annwyn (pronounced* **anoon**) *in the hope of meeting the spirits of the beloved dead.* ❞

ENERGY RAISING

★ Chant:

❝ *Danu, Sulis, Rhiannon, Brighid, Cerridwen, Morgan, Epona.* ❞

★ Repeat at least nine times.

EPONA EVOCATION

❝ *Epona, Horse Goddess of the Celtic people, who rides on Albion's fair hills, we ask you to join us in our ritual, to protect our circle and us therein from any malign or mischievous spirits that enter from Gwyn ab Nud's underworld castle.* ❞

RIGHT: *A priest extinguishes the temple candles with his athame. He leaves a single candle burning on the altar—to be extinguished later by Gwyn ap Nud's invoker.*

TOP: *Epona, the Horse Goddess, is asked to "protect the circle and its occupants from any malign or mischievous spirits that enter from Gwyn ab Nud's underworld castle."*

ABOVE: *Before the advent of electric light winters were hard to endure. Ghosts and demons roamed freely in the darkness. Samhain is the gateway to winter.*

★ All candles are extinguished with the athame except for one on the altar.

★ The god is invoked in the west quarter.

GWYN AB NUD INVOCATION

66 Dread Lord, who rules in the halls of the dead, Gwyn ab Nud, who leads the dancers in the castle under the hill, speak to us. Take away our fear of death, come to us, through the body of this thy priest and servant, who loves you. 99

GWYN AP NUD CHARGE

66 I hold the treasure house of the past. The old ones gather at my shoulder—workers with flint and bronze and iron—all those who made you what you are. Listen to them, your ancestors. You have forgotten much that they knew. 99

★ The priest who is Gwyn ap Nud moves to sit in the northwest.

★ The high priestess cuts a doorway in the west with her athame, saying:

66 Gwyn ap Nud, we ask you to open wide the gates to Annwyn through which we all shall pass one day. We welcome, to our ritual, the spirits of our loved ones who are in the underworld and any others who offer us no harm or illwill. 99

★ The invoker extinguishes the last candle with her athame, saying:

66 Summer is dead. We feast with death. 99

★ All sit and commune with the spirits.

★ When she feels the time is right, the high priestess rises and lights all the temple candles.

AU REVOIR TO GWYN AB NUD

66 Gwyn ab Nud, we thank you for attending our rite. We ask you now to depart from our priest, your servant, and allow him to return to the world of men. Hail and farewell. 99

★ The doorway in the northwest is closed by the high priestess.

★ Cakes and wine.

★ This is a time to use your divinatory skills—especially looking in the black mirror and crystal ball. All play party games, for example, bobbing for apples.

★ Close the circle.

Midwinter Solstice Ritual

The midwinter solstice—or Yule—*is celebrated on December 21–22. It is the longest night of the year and the worst of winter still lies ahead, so a festival of lights and feasting is a psychological necessity. Wiccans deck their houses with holly and ivy and feast like many other people at this time of year.*

PREPARATION

★ Deck the temple with Yuletide greenery.

★ Find a dark cloak or cloth—this is needed to cover Horus.

★ Cast the circle, using the midwinter opening invocation below.

★ Salute the quarters as usual.

OPENING INVOCATION

❝*Hail to thee most high mistress of divine magic. Speak unto our hearts the secret words of Thoth. Make our hearts know joy, which is thee, O Sweet one, for you are the Nile. Fertile silt travels up to the black lands, to the wearer of the red crown, to Wadjet, the hooded one. Mighty Isis, bring forth the child the Earth has been waiting for.*❞

ENERGY RAISING

★ Chant:

❝*Re, Horakhty" (Ray–hor–aka–tay).*❞

★The priest who is to be invoked is covered by a dark cloth.

ISIS INVOCATION

❝*Come, most beautiful, you who are more seductive than any enchantress, you who whisper to the hearts of men. O come, mother of this world. Come, Queen Isis, you who are the stars amid the heavens. For you the sun doth shine and the moon beams her brilliance. Come to us, Great One, speak to us, descend unto your priestess who loves you truly.*❞

BELOW: *The scribe Ani kneels before Osiris in this scene from the* Egyptian Book of the Dead. *The hawk-headed god Horus acts as Ani's guide and protector.*

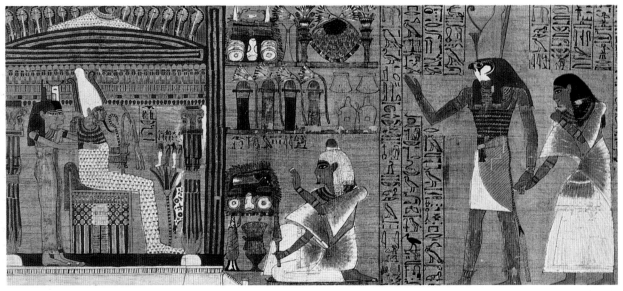

ISIS CHARGE

❝ I heard your voice amid the outer limits of time and space, as my body shook with longing and the pain of birth. I am the mother of all life. I was created and I am the creator; I am mistress of birth and death. I bring forth the Lord of Life, the child of Osiris, who abides in the land of the blessed, beyond the western hills; he is life in death, as I am death in life. I am Isis, the rising one held high. ❞

HORUS INVOCATION

❝ Heket, Goddess of Frogs and the Power of Life Magic, blow the breath of life into Horus. Meskhent, Goddess of Birth and Destiny, Lady of Fate and Fortune, lay your blessing upon Horus, Lord of Earth. ❞

★ The invoker removes the cloth, and Horus stands.

★ The invoker kneels and continues:

❝ Come Lord Horus, born unto our land, shine your face onto your people. You who are the son of our hearts, come glorious of face, come Earth's Lord. Speak to us now. Descend into your priest, who loves you truly. ❞

ABOVE: *The invoking priestess removes the dark cloth, Horus stands, and she concludes the invocation. He promises: "I, who am the power of the sun, will brighten with each day."*

HORUS CHARGE

❝ I, who am the power of the sun, will brighten with each day. I bring hope for an abundant future harvest, a time of prosperity. I am the righter of wrongs. I can be cruel to the cruelest, and loving to the lowly. I am the Lord of this world. I am the jewel within the crown of Isis. I am hope and joy, life and love. I am the eye of the day and the eye of the night that shine their brilliance onto the land of men. ❞

★ Horus and Isis embrace.
★ Their invokers earth them with an embrace.
★ All sit in a circle holding hands.
★ The priestess stands in the east and lights a white candle, saying:

❝ Our Lord, the child of light, has returned to us. ❞

★ The priestess places the candle in the center of the group.
★ All meditate upon the light.
★ Cakes and wine.
★ Close the circle.

> ### SOURCE
>
> This material is from *The Birth of Horus*, written by Lesley Dennet, High Priestess of Nut–Horus.

First Degree Initiation Ritual

Initiation into a coven is not to be entered into lightly. It is a transformative experience that makes you confront your inner demons before helping your rebirth into the light. First degree is initiation of the personality, which involves an element of ordeal or hazing. Initiation is between an individual and their gods and goddesses; all a coven can do is to admit the person to their working group. It is an inner process that outward ritual merely facilitates.

PREPARATION

★ Procure a mirror that is large enough to hide the priest holding it from the initiate.

★ The initiate should procure some three-yard long cords (*see* Tools) that are red, white, and blue. The ends of the cords should not be knotted—use adhesive tape to stop them from fraying.

★ The initiate is told that they will be asked what they are during the ritual and that they should answer "a witch."

★ The initiate will also need to decide on a spirit name before the ritual begins.

★ The initiate makes a request to the temple gods and goddesses to be accepted to the temple. Discuss the words to be used with the initiate before the ritual.

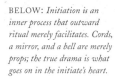

BELOW: *Initiation is an inner process that outward ritual merely facilitates. Cords, a mirror, and a bell are merely props; the true drama is what goes on in the initiate's heart.*

THE RITUAL

★ The initiate is sent into a separate room to prepare.

★ Do not rush to collect him or her; give them time to meditate on what they are letting themselves in for.

★ They are collected by a priest and priestess, robed and looking stern, who treat them as a stranger.

★ Everyone else is standing, silently, in the temple in the hope that the initiate will not know they are there.

★ The high priestess stands to the side of the initiate, holding a bell.

★ At the door of the temple the initiate is challenged by a priest(ess), who says:

❝ *When you are initiated, you are initiated into your own strength—which is the strength of the Earth and the ancestors—of sun and moon and of all the powers that lie ranked beyond them, up to the last unknowable One, which we call Dryghten. You bind yourself to no man and no woman but to the gods and goddesses of your own heart, and they will teach you the craft of the wise, which is no secret (though some would make it so) but the sum total of all that you are. It should not be given for money, but freely and for the love of the gods. You stand at the secret door. Look into your heart and*

answer truly; are you ready to serve the god and goddess as an initiate of this temple and to walk, with us, between the worlds? 99

★ The initiate replies.
★ The priest(ess) then asks: "What is your name?"
★ The initiate gives their spirit name.
★ Blindfold the initiate.
★ Take the initiate into the temple; he or she faces north.
★ The priests who collected them make a noise leaving the temple. (The initiate should think they are alone and be startled by the bell.)
★ All stand silently for a few minutes.
★ The high priestess rings the bell, close to initiate, and the others return.
★ Turn the initiate to face south—just in front of the altar but not touching it.
★ Everyone arranges themselves around the initiate to form a circle.
★ All the women and then all the men stand in front of the initiate and, in turn, hold the initiate's hands and introduce themselves. Use spirit names and the following formula:

66 *I am Morrigan, the Washer at the Ford.* 99 (Your name.)

66 *I help you to leave behind that which is no longer needed.* 99 (What you do.)

66 *I give you the strength to examine and overcome your innermost fears.* 99 (Your gift to the initiate.)

★ Bind the initiate with the cords.
★ The first cord is used to fasten their hands together behind their back and is looped around their neck—not too tight but not too loose.
★ The second cord binds the initiate around the knees.
★ The third cord is tied loosely around their ankles—tuck the ends in so the initiate will not trip.
★ Place the initiate in the northwest corner.
★ Cast the circle, using the opening invocation below.
★ Salute the elements.

ABOVE: *The blindfolded initiate is placed facing south, in front of the altar but not touching it. Everybody in turn takes the initiate's hands and introduces themselves using their spirit names.*

OPENING INVOCATION

 God and goddess spin the web of life for all living things, with many paths for us to choose from. Let us feel their love in our hearts. Let us walk our parallel paths, learning from one another in perfect love and perfect trust. Blessed be.

ENERGY RAISING

★ Chant, using the names of the particular temple deities.

GOD AND GODDESS

★ Use your temple god and goddess for invocations and charges.

★ The priest(ess) cuts a doorway in the northwest and stands before the initiate, with the sword leveled at, and touching, the initiate's breast and says:

 (Spirit name), *again and for the last time you stand separate from us, do you now wish to be accepted as an initiate of* (temple deities)?

★ The initiate replies.

★ The high priest(ess) asks:

 Do you enter this circle with perfect love and perfect trust? Do you wish to learn to work with and for your goddess and god?

Do you promise never to bring any ill will into the circle?

ABOVE: *After a doorway is cut in the northwest a priestess levels the sword at the initiate's breast, challenges him or her, and then kisses them over the threshold.*

★ As each question is answered the bell is rung three times.

★ The high priest(ess) puts down the sword, turns to the initiate and says:

 Join us.

★ The high priest(ess) then kisses the initiate over the threshold and stands him or her in the center.

★ The doorway is closed.

★ The high priest(ess) kneels before the initiate and says:

 Are you willing to swear your intent and be purified?

★ Jostle and spin the initiate.

★ Asperge (anoint) the initiate with water.

★ Remove the cords.

★ A priest holds the mirror in front of the initiate.

★ A priestess stands directly behind the initiate and says:

 You stand in the presence of the one who judges truly and knows the secrets of your heart. You must now make your solemn undertaking in the Art Magical.

★ Remove the blindfold and step away, so that all the initiate sees is his or her own face reflected in the mirror.

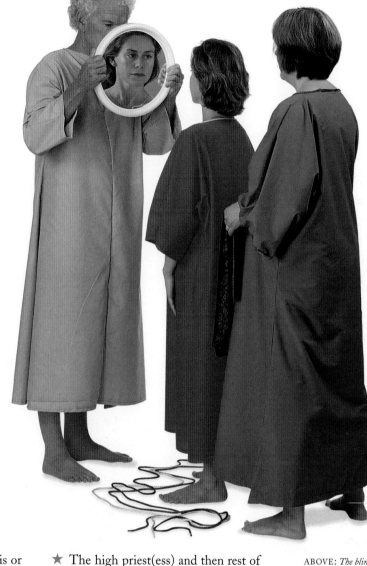

★ The priest holding mirror says:

“Declare before your judge; what are you?”

★ The initiate replies:

“I am a witch.”

★ The question and reply are made three times.

★ The initiate is helped to kneel before the altar. The high priest(ess) says:

“(Spirit name), it is time for you to ask (temple god and goddess) to accept you as their priest(ess).”

★ The initiate makes the request in his or her own words. These should have been discussed earlier.

★ The high priest(ess) says:

“You agree to dedicate this lifetime to the craft. Many things and many people will try to break your resolution. Remember, your power comes from within. Listen to others, be quick to help and slow to judge. In all things be guided by your goddesses and gods. Always remember the Wiccan Rede, 'An it harm none do what you will.' As newly made priest(ess) you are equal to all in this temple. I now salute you in the most sacred names of (temple god and goddess), newly made priest(ess) of this temple.”

★ The high priest(ess) and then rest of coven embrace and welcome the initiate.

★ The high priest and high priestess, on either side of the initiate, take him or her to the four quarters and proclaim:

“Brothers and sisters of (the east etc.). We present to you (name), who is a priest(ess) of this temple. We ask you to guard, guide, and make him/her welcome.”

★ Cakes and wine.
★ Initiation presents are given.
★ Close the circle.

ABOVE: *The blindfold is removed and all the initiate can see is her own face reflected in the mirror. She is then asked who she is, and she declares: "I am a witch."*

Second Degree Initiation Ritual

Second degree is initiation of the spirit. It is tailored to the individual and contains an element of surprise; it is often spoken of as the dark night of the soul. You will be launched down a hard and lonely path, during which you will need all your wits about you. Wait for a period in your life when you feel settled in yourself and your relationships before you test yourself in this way. This sounds discouraging, but remember—the harder the path, the better the homecoming.

MYTHIC DRAMA

One way of celebrating second degree is through the enactment of a brief mythic drama. The initiate plays the role of a goddess, god, or hero whose quest takes them into the underworld. For a woman, the legend of Inanna would be appropriate; for a man, the myth of Odin and the runes. The initiate is interrogated by the invoked god or goddess, as in the example that follows.

BELOW: *The initiate comes to the ritual with three yards each of purple and silver cords. The colors are chosen to evoke the night sky and starlight.*

PREPARATION

★ The initiate should procure three yards each of purple and silver cords. Do not knot the ends.

★ Usually the initiate will change his or her spirit name.

★ The coven club together to buy the initiate a ring.

THE RITUAL

★ Cast the circle.

★ Salute the elements.

★ Perform an appropriate energy-raising chant.

★ Challenge the initiate to state their request for initiation. This can replace the opening invocation.

INVOCATION

Invoke only a god or goddess. This deity will act as the initiate's interrogator. If the Inanna myth is enacted, then the Underworld goddess Ereshkigal is invoked. If the Odin myth is used, then Odin himself is the interrogator.

ABOVE: *In Sumarian myth Inanna descends into the Underworld to confront her sister Erishkigal. She is stripped and hung from a hook for three days before returning to life.*

THE INTERROGATION

This is an example of the interrogation using the Inanna myth. The initiate is wearing a robe, cords, and a crown of flowers, but has not yet been told their significance.

★ The initiate faces the interrogator in the north.
★ Erishkigal says:

66 You are Inanna the supplicant. Render to me your robes—for none needs clothing in the land of the dead. 99

★ Erishkigal's assistants take the robe and throw it aside. Pause while this is done.

66 Render to me your crown of flowers—for all is barren in the land of the dead. 99

★ Erishkigal's assistants take the crown of flowers and throw it aside. Pause while this is done.

66 Render to me your cords—for none has status in the land of the dead. 99

★ Erishkigal's assistants take the cords and contemptuously throw them aside. Pause while this is done.

66 Now I take from you the light of life. No friend can help you, no star can guide you, for you are alone in the land of the dead. Sit and watch in the halls of the dead. 99

★ Extinguish all the candles.
★ Everyone except the initiate leaves the temple. After a few minutes all go back in and sit quietly. When it feels right, the candles are lit again.
★ Give Inanna a single feather, saying:

66 You are Inanna, the owl who flies in the dark. 99

★ Give Inanna a lit candle, with the words:

66 You are Inanna, the owl who sees in the dark. 99

★ Give Inanna the ring, with the words:

66 You are Inanna, the owl who is sealed to the dark. 99

★ All embrace and congratulate the candidate.
★ Take the candidate to each quarter and introduce them as high priest(ess).
★ Cakes and wine.
★ Close the circle.

ABOVE: *Inanna is associated with the owl, the wise bird that sees and hunts in the dark. The initiate, just like Inanna, must face her own darkness to gain wisdom.*

Third Degree Initiation Ritual

Third degree initiation is really a ritual of farewell. It is a final dotting of i's and crossing of t's, and an acknowledgement that the initiate is now ready to be running a group totally separate from their mother coven. The status of the initiate vis-a-vis the mother coven should be negotiated in advance. Some covens break all contact after third degree, others accept the initiate as a visiting priest(ess) at every sabbat or even every ritual.

The writing of the ritual is often set as a third-degree task. It is the initiate's final opportunity to show what they know. Usually they also do the lion's share of the work in the ritual. Where first and second degree contain elements of surprise and ordeal, third degree is a celebration of the initiate's achievement.

PREPARATION

★ The initiate should purchase, and wear, three yards of gold cord—again, do not tie knots at the ends.

★ The initiate may be asked to take the group on a pathworking or lead a workshop, before or during the ritual.

★ Cast the circle, using an appropriate opening invocation.

★ Salute the elements.

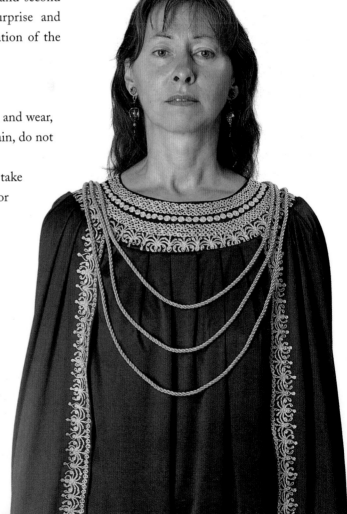

RIGHT: *At third degree the initiate proudly wears three yards of gold cord. Gold, the color of the sun, and long regarded as the most precious of metals, symbolizes achievement.*

ENERGY RAISING

This poem, *Eldorado* by Edgar Allen Poe, is suitable for energy raising at both second and third degree initiation rituals.

1 Gaily bedight,
A gallant knight
In sunshine and in shadow,
Had journeyed long,
Singing a song,
In search of Eldorado

2 But he grew old—
This knight so bold—
And o'er his heart a shadow
Fell as he found
No spot of ground
That looked like Eldorado

3 And, as his strength
Failed him at length,
He met a pilgrim shadow—
"Shadow," said he,
"Where can it be—
This land of Eldorado?"

4 "Over the Mountains
Of the Moon,
Down the Valley of the Shadow,
Ride, boldly ride,"
The shade replied—
"If you seek for Eldorado."

OPENING INVOCATION

There is no challenge in this ritual; the initiate is already established as a high priest(ess) of the coven. The opening invocation thanks the gods for all that the person has done and asks them for their continued blessing. This is a beginning as well as an ending.

INVOCATIONS AND CHARGES

By the third degree the initiate is on the way toward the integration of their personality. A way of marking this is to invoke the initiate as both goddess and god. They charge as one before being invoked as the other.

★ After the initiate is earthed, the high priest(ess) embraces him or her and says:

66 *The bonds are broken, the cords are cut, come and go in perfect freedom and perfect love.* 99

★ He or she then opens curtains at the window of the temple (if practicable) and says:

66 *There is your temple.* 99

★ All embrace the initiate.
★ The initiate is taken around the quarters and their new status proclaimed.
★ Cakes and wine.
★ Presents are then given as appropriate.
★ Close the circle.

BELOW: *After blessing cakes and wine, the initiate can relax. They have shown the coven that they are competent in all aspects of ritual.*

How to do Spells

Spells are prayers with attitude. Intent is all-important. The things you use in magic—chants, candles, talismans, cords—are there only to help you focus your intent. They are like the personal props an actor uses to get himself into character. Be clear about what you want. You may be looking for a specific result—for example, the healing of a particular medical condition; or you may simply be sending a person love and good wishes—like a "Get Well" card. The more specific your objective, the more careful you have to be about precise targeting.

ABOVE: *To make a spell you have to raise energy. The cone of power raised in a ritual may suffice, but you will probably need to do more chanting and dancing.*

MAKING THE SPELL

There are many different ways of making and sending spells (as shown overleaf in Some Useful Spells). Once you have done a few, you will find your own preferred methods. The essential thing is to raise energy. If you are working within a ritual, the energy banked when you raised the cone of power may suffice, but more probably you will want to supplement it with more dancing, chanting, or exercises in mental concentration. You then have to will or wish the energy into your spell. You can transfer it to a person or object by touch or, if the target is at a distance, by visualizing its passage through the ether.

MAGICAL LINK

Almost anything can be used as a tool in spellcraft. Your intent can be carried by a

form of words or transmitted through a physical object, such as a candle or a talisman. You need to create a magical link between yourself and your target. You can carry this off simply by thinking hard, but the use of an object makes the thinking easier. Absent healing can be carried out using a doll or puppet that has been chosen to represent the individual.

Photographs can be used either as alternatives to dolls or as aids to visualization.

SYMBOLIC ASSOCIATIONS

When choosing your tools you need to be sensitive to their symbolic associations. Metals, precious stones, spices, and herbs exist within a web of magical correspondence. Iron, for example, is associated with the planet Mars and has long been used in magic for the making of protective amulets. Fairies and other supernatural beings are supposedly allergic to it. Iron objects might, therefore, be used in a protective spell, but not in a spell invoking supernatural help.

The car protection talisman on page 115 contains a number of herbs chosen for their magical associations. Each herb has a particular job to do. They are contained within a red sachet because red is the color of full-blooded life, alertness and self-assertion. These martial qualities are controlled by the white cord, because white is the color of purity and peace. The driver of the car in question can remain calm, relaxed, and alert, knowing that the sachet is working positively on his or her behalf.

LEFT: *You need to create a magical link between yourself and the target of your spell. A doll or picture gives you something to focus on in absent healing.*

Some Useful Spells

Spells require forethought and preparation as well as a great deal of energy, so make sure you have everything you need for the spell before you raise energy for the cone of power and be aware of how much energy you are going to have to "withdraw" from the cone.

BACK TO BACK

★ All members of the coven sit in a circle, backs touching, facing outward.

★ You formulate the object of your spell in a chant containing one word more or less than the number of people in the circle. For example, five people are doing a spell to help Blake pass his exams. This means you need a six- or four-word phrase, for example, "Blake–remembers–his–learning–in–exams." (Blake of course has to have done his studying and homework for the spell to work.)

★ Starting with the person who knows Blake best, each person, working sunwise, says one word of the chant.

★ Begin slowly and get progressively faster.

★ Everyone starts the chant three times.

★ The person who started the chant then sends the energy to Blake.

★ When you have done this, say:
❝ *So mote it be.* ❞

WEALTH

Consecrate a coin during a ritual, put it in with your other money, and it will attract more coins of the same value.

BELOW: *In a Back to Back spell, a sentence is passed around the circle one word at a time. The sentence contains one word more or less than there are people.*

A GATEWAY SPELL

A gateway spell is used to send positive energy to a distant place that needs it, for example, you might send energy to a war zone or an area of ecological disaster.

★ Choose an item (an ornament or shell, for example).

★ Consecrate it.

★ Visualize it as a gateway to the place you wish to help.

★ Think of it as a one-way route (you do not want negative energies to come back at you).

★ Place it on your altar, saying:

66 *Here is a gateway to* (place-name). *All excess energies raised here will go to* (place-name) *through this gateway and correct what is wrong.* 99

This spell will hold until you "deactivate" the gateway by deconsecrating it (*see pages 84–85*).

ABOVE: *An everyday object such as a shell can become a gateway through which, over a period of time, you send magical energy to a distant target.*

CAR TALISMAN

★ Onto a square of red cloth put these herbs or plants:

• One teaspoon comfrey and one and a half teaspoons mugwort (for protection during travel)

• One teaspoon caraway (for protection against theft)

• One and half teaspoons rosemary (for alertness)

• One tablespoon ash tree bark (for protection against accidents)

• Ten drops lavender oil (to refresh talisman when smell fades)

★ Tie the cloth into a bundle with a white cord and suspend it in the car.

CANDLE MAGIC

Candles release their energy slowly and are particularly effective for influencing emotional and mental states. They function rather like slow-release medicine. They can either be lit in the temple or given to the client to burn when needed.

If used in the temple, a candle is passed around the group and each person adds his or her own energies. You might also apply an appropriate oil.

A helpful insignia can be carved into the candle using the white-handled knife. For example, to counter fear of flying, take a blue candle and carve a small figure of an airplane into it.

ABOVE: *A simple talisman can be made by mixing herbs, oils, spices, and gums and tying them up with white cord in a red cloth bag.*

Be careful in selecting the color of the candle. If someone is depressed and you choose a red candle for them they could become destructive. A sunny yellow candle would be better.

ABOVE: *Essential oils are distilled to concentrate the goodness in flowers, herbs, and resins. They are 100% pure and a few drops are all that is needed to energize a bath.*

LOVE MAGIC

Love magic is about making you, or your friend, feel lovable. For this you need to be relaxed, unstressed—and to love yourself.

Before an evening out:

★ Light a yellow candle in your bathroom.

★ Run a warm/hot bath.

★ Add some of these oils: gardenia, lavender, lemon verbena, rose, vanilla, lime, patchouli, or ylang ylang.

★ Lie back and soak for between fifteen and thirty minutes.

To relax and invigorate yourself:

★ Light a blue candle.

★ Sit or lie in a comfortable and warm position, with the candle in front of you.

★ Do not cross legs or arms, because this restricts the energy flow.

★ Breathing evenly and deeply, close your eyes and concentrate on your muscles.

★ Relax the toes in your right foot, then the left. Your toes will feel heavy.

★ Let the muscles in your feet become heavy and relaxed.

★ Slowly concentrating on each in turn, relax the muscles of your feet, legs, stomach, back, shoulders, arms, hands, and neck.

★ Move upward to your skull; relax the muscles of your face and head.

★ Open your eyes and look into the candle flame; picture yourself in the flame, relaxed, smiling, and enjoying yourself.

★ When you feel yourself to be as relaxed as your image of yourself, stand up and stretch.

★ Your body will tingle with warm, invigorating energy.

LOVE INCENSE

This powerful mixture is to burn in the bathroom, to aid relaxation, before you go out or while you are getting ready. Add together:

• Two parts sandalwood

• A half part basil

• A half part bergamot

• A few drops of two of the oils mentioned under Love Magic.

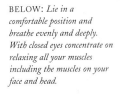

BELOW: *Lie in a comfortable position and breathe evenly and deeply. With closed eyes concentrate on relaxing all your muscles including the muscles on your face and head.*

HOME PROTECTION SACHETS

To help protect your home, wrap the following ingredients in red cloth and pin the bundle to the inner side of external doors:

- One tablespoon each nettle (herb) and either cedarwood or sandalwood (for physical protection)
- Two bay leaves (for psychic awareness)
- Ten drops of frankincense oil (to deter unwanted entry)
- Ten drops of tangerine oil (to give you the power to keep unwanted visitors out)
- A few drops of patchouli or violet oils or a few menthol crystals can also be added.

PERSONAL PROTECTION

Have you ever noticed that you can be feeling happy and relaxed, but if you mix with anxious, stressed-out people (for example, on a train or when shopping), you start to feel as they do? You are picking up their vibrations. One-to-one you could keep your equanimity, but a crowd may overpower you.

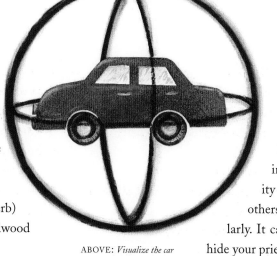

ABOVE: *Visualize the car you will be traveling in and mentally using your sword or athame surround it with three circles in order to to protect it against theft and accident.*

What you need is a suit of armor. Close your eyes and picture yourself totally encased in a suit of steel. If you like, you can make it so that instead of just blunting negativity it radiates cheerfulness to others. You need to renew this regularly. It can also be used if you want to hide your priestly light for a while.

PSYCHIC PROTECTION

If you feel yourself under psychic attack and want to defend yourself without hurling your own psychic thunderbolts, give your suit of armor a mirrorlike surface, which reflects all unwanted energy back where it came from.

THREE CIRCLES

An easy way of creating temporary protection wherever you are (for example, traveling in a car without a talisman, or on vacation and wanting to protect your belongings) is to mentally use your sword or athame to draw three circles around what you want to protect. You mentally touch the points where the three circles cross with golden light (using a sword or athame) to energize them.

A HEALING RUNE

To be chanted while circling, with the person to be healed, or a representative, in the center:

f *This is the spell that we intone,*
Flesh to flesh and bone to bone,
Sinew to sinew and vein to vein,
And each one will be whole again. ™

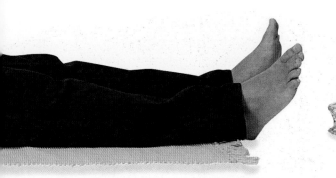

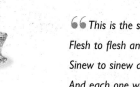

Pathworking

A pathworking is a guided meditation that takes you on a journey through a symbolic inner landscape. It is a structured and purposeful daydream. The narrative will always allow the walker time and space to interact with the landscape and its inhabitants. Pathworkings are a way of exploring the self.

THE RIGHT FRAME OF MIND

Pathworkings are a good way of getting yourself into the right frame of mind for ritual. Let people sit or lie in comfortable positions around the temple, with their eyes shut. The pathworking should be familiar to the narrator and spoken from memory—nothing disrupts a pathworking as much as the rustle of paper. Sometimes things will turn up on the path that were absent last time it was walked, and the leader needs to be able to improvize without losing control.

If done within ritual a pathworking should have some relevance to what is to follow. For example, at Imbolc a pathworking might lead through bare woods to meet Jack-in-the-Green. A coven that is starting up might want to preface each of its rituals with a version of the same pathworking as a way of building up the group mind; this is then shortened each time until it is no longer needed because the coven clicks into the right mindset as soon as its members enter the temple. When there are new members, it should be done a couple of times to ease the new members into the group.

FOLLOW THE SAFETY CODE

Explorations of the inner realm can have a profound effect, and the leader must be prepared to deal with the emotions that arise.

RIGHT: *You are on a narrow path in a wood. You look to the left and the right and you see all kinds of wild animals running up the hill.*

It is important that the walkers know that they are safe and that any nightmarish qualities on the path are easily banished.

Walkers need to be led gently onto the path and gently off of it at the other end. Sometimes unanticipated problems will arise concerning people's phobias. For example, someone with a fear of birds is likely to have a panic attack if she is told she is sprouting

wings and taking off through the air. The leader is like a tour guide; he or she must walk the path while keeping a close eye on his or her charges.

BEGINNING AND END

A good way to begin a pathworking is to surround the walkers with a colored mist that slowly clears to reveal the symbolic landscape. At the end of the path, you bring the mist back down and tell the walkers that they are returning "to this place and this time."

THE WASHER AT THE FORD

The pathworking that follows is an allegory of initiation. Prepare for people to be disorientated by their experience at the stream and give them time to recover. When the god and goddess speak, allow plenty of time for each person to hear their message and interact with them. Do not be surprised if the pathworking throws in something different each time it is done.

SETTING OUT

Close your eyes, breathe evenly and deeply; you are warm, comfortable, and safe. A bright golden mist swirls all around you. The mist clears, and you are on a narrow path in a wood; it is late afternoon and there is a warm breeze. The path rises gently. You look to the left and the right and you see all kinds of wild animals running up the hill. There is no animosity between hunter and hunted. You hear indistinct, merry music—pipes being played. You walk up the hill, toward the music. *(The storyteller pauses.)*

WALK WITH THE ANIMALS

When you reach the top the path dips gently downward. The animals are still around you. Here and there are larger animals, animals from the farmyard, pets, horses, and ponies. You carry on walking down the path. *(Pause.)* Before you is a stream. There is a figure washing bloody cloths in the stream where the animals are crossing. The animals acknowledge the presence of this person, who is hooded and cloaked. You cannot see whether it is male or female, young or old. You arrive at the stream. *(Pause.)*

INTO THE WATER

The figure turns toward you, but the hood still covers its face. It raises its left arm and points a bony finger across the water. The sound of the pipes is louder. The animals scamper out of the way, and you set foot into the stream. After a couple of steps, the water suddenly rises up and swamps you, knocking you off your feet. *(Pause.)* You do not know which way is up. Panic rises inside, and your lungs are burning. Then the water just as suddenly subsides and gently carries you to the farther shore. *(Pause.)*

THE BLACK CROW

You look back; the figure has gone. The animals are crossing again, and they scamper past you. You reach up and take hold of a great standing stone and haul yourself out of the water. A large black crow lands on the stone and gives a loud "caw." You move forward. A white horse passes you. The crow flies from the stone and lands on the horse's

BELOW: *A large black crow gives a loud caw. A white horse passes you by. The crow flies from the stone and lands on the horse's back.*

120

back. The path is steep, leading up a grassy hillside. The music is getting louder and clearer. *(Pause.)*

THE PIPER AND THE LADY

You reach the top of the hill. The path passes over the top and into a hollow where there is a stone circle. All the animals are here, frolicking, running, or just sitting and listening to the music. In the center of the circle is a man with shaggy thighs; he is playing panpipes and has a crow perched on his left shoulder. He looks at you as you enter the stone circle and winks at you. His eyes are merry and bright, his face ready for laughter. The crow launches itself into the air, and you watch it

momentarily. You look to the man again and by his side is a beautiful, mature woman wearing a crown of flowers. She starts to sing. You sit with your back to one of the stones, and watch the animals, who each touch the woman's hand as they pass.

THE RETURN

The man stops playing his pipes and beckons to you. You walk across to him and the beautiful woman; they embrace you and each of them speaks to you. *(Longer pause.)* You return to your seat. The music and singing begin again. You close your eyes, and the golden mist envelops you and returns you to this place and this time.

ABOVE: *In the center of the circle is a man with shaggy thighs; he is playing panpipes and has a crow perched on his left shoulder.*

121

4 | Wicca in the Twenty-first Century

As the millennium dawns, modern Wicca celebrates its fiftieth anniversary. Gardner's books appeared in a world still recovering from the Second World War. Harry S. Truman was President and Joseph Stalin was still in charge in Russia. Gardnerian Wicca is essentially a religion of the mid-twentieth century. In its romanticism, its frank sexuality, its hankering after a mythical golden age it can be seen as a protest against the twentieth century's drabbest and most conformist decade. Gardner's work has echoes in J.R.R. Tolkien's Lord of the Rings—*another product of the 1950s.*

The signs are that Gardner did not expect Wicca to catch on. He saw himself as an antiquarian recording a dying religion before it finally disappeared. He was wrong. Wiccan spirituality caught the mood of the 1960s, and from there on went from strength to strength. In the 1970s it happily embraced feminism. In the 1980s it found itself in sympathy with the ideals and philosophies of the New Age. In the 1990s it was in accord with the environmental movement and alive to the possibilities of cyberspace. At the turn of the century it is arguably the fastest growing religion of the age.

Wicca's adaptability stands it in good stead. Unencumbered by holy books or fixed dogma, it has the potential to grow and change with the Aquarian Age. Provided humanity keeps its nerve, the new millennium could see us fulfilling our wildest dreams: Space travel, longevity stretching out to virtual immortality, time travel, and freedom from disease could all be within our grasp. Wiccans, believing as they do that the divine is within us, are unfazed by the prospect of human beings becoming like gods and goddesses.

Do-It-Yourself Wicca

The one thing Wicca is never likely to become is a mass movement. Wiccans work in small groups or on their own—or both. They need to be flexible and to recognize that there are no absolute rights and wrongs. Styles of working differ. There is only one mountain, but any number of different routes up it. Wicca is a religion for individualists—a do-it-yourself religion.

THE POWER OF WICCA

Be true to yourself and your principles. Do not do anything you would be ashamed of. If anyone asks you to do something you are not comfortable with, do not do it. If a spell feels a little "gray," either try to do it a different way or forget about it. The practice of Wicca gives you power; be careful not to abuse it. There is nothing wrong with keeping your religion a secret—after all, Wiccans do not proselytize—but do not let it be a guilty secret. You are the priest or priestess of your goddesses and gods; aim to be their worthy representative.

THE LIVING WORLD

When devising spells and rituals be sensitive to the living world around you. Nature does not go by calendars, so

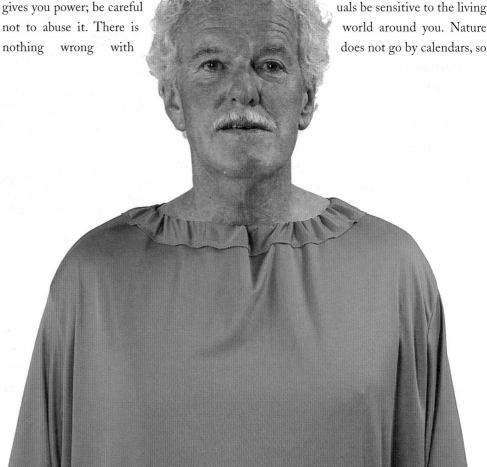

RIGHT: *Wicca is a religion for individualists. It is a do-it-yourself religion. You are the priest or priestess of your goddesses and gods. Be their worthy representative.*

avoid devising anything too far in advance. There is no sense in rhapsodizing about spring flowers and singing birds if it is snowing outside. Be open to surprises. The best rituals and spells are often those in which you lose sight of the script and let the gods and goddesses take over.

MIRTH AND REVERENCE

Do not take yourself too seriously. Treat the goddesses and gods with respect but not with superstitious awe. Remember that they are part of you and you are part of them. They have as much of a sense of humor as you do. Some of the things you do in the circle are intrinsically funny; do not repress your laughter as inappropriate. Nothing raises more energy or does more to build a group mind than laughter. The Wiccan watchwords are "mirth and reverence."

DIVINE WILL

Every day is sacred to Wiccans, and every mundane action is an act of worship. For Wiccans there is no separation between the physical and the spiritual; both are one. Look around you now: everything you see, the walls of the room, the view from the window, people, plants, animals, are expressions of the divine will. So too are the institutions, technologies and media that support life in the 21st century. Neither nature nor the man-made world is particularly benign. The gods and goddesses are blind forces who work through our eyes, hands, and minds. Wicca is not a religion of escape, but a way of engaging with reality—a way of life and a state of mind.

BE CREATIVE

This book has given you the basics for a "book of shadows." It is a launch pad. The heart of Wicca is the individual's relationship with the gods and goddesses. Allow them to inspire you and take you further. Explore your own creativity.

ABOVE: *The world outside the window is your temple. Be sensitive to the living things around you. Nature does not go by calendars, so avoid devising rituals too far in advance.*

Further Reading

Adler, Margot. *Drawing Down the Moon.* Beacon, 1986.

Apuleius, Lucius. *Golden Ass.* Chapters 4 and 5. Translated by Robert Graves. Penguin, 1990.

Basford, Kathleen. *The Green Man.* Ipswich, 1978.

Cohn, Norman. *Europe's Inner Demons.* Basic Books, 1975.

Crowley, Vivianne. *Wicca, The Old Religion in the New Age.* Aquarian, 1989.

Crowley, Vivianne. *Phoenix from the Flame.* Aquarian, 1990.

Eliot, T.S. *Little Gidding*, Section 1. From: *Complete Poems and Plays of T.S. Eliot.* Faber & Faber, 1969.

Farrar, Janet and Stewart. *Eight Sabbats for Witches.* Hale, 1981.

Farrar, Janet and Stewart. *The Witches Way.* Hale, 1990.

Frazer, Sir James. *The Golden Bough.* Macmillan, 1922.

Gardner, Gerald. *Witchcraft Today.* Rider, 1954.

Gardner, Gerald. *The Meaning of Witchcraft.* Rider, 1959.

Graves, Robert. *The White Goddess.* Faber & Faber, 1948.

Kipling, Rudyard. *Puck of Pook's Hill.* Macmillan, 1906.

Miller, Ronald. *The Green Man.* SB Publications, 1998.

Macleod, Fiona. *The Washer at the Ford.* Patrick Geddes & Co., 1896.

Moxon, E. *Wordsworth's Poetical Works.* 1843.

Murray, Margaret. *The Witch Cult in Western Europe.* Oxford University Press, 1921.

Murray, Margaret. *The God of the Witches.* Sampson Low, Marston & Co., 1933.

Poe, Edgar Allen. *Complete Stories and Poems.* Doubleday, 1966.

Starhawk (Miriam Simos). *The Spiral Dance.* Harper & Row, 1979.

Starhawk (Miriam Simos). *Dreaming the Dark.* Beacon Press, 1982.

Starhawk (Miriam Simos). *Truth or Dare.* HarperCollins, 1987.

Suzuki, D.T. *Essays in Zen Buddhism.* Rider, 1949.

Yeats, W.B. *Collected Poems.* Macmillan, 1950.

Glossary

Athame: Black-handled knife

Black mirror: Used for scrying; it does not give a definite reflection

Cakes and wine: Symbolic Great Rite (lovemaking)

Casting the circle: All the actions involved in creating an energized circle, i.e., sweeping the circle, taking a candle around to fill the circle with light

Censer: Implement, such as a dish containing sand or earth, in which charcoal can be burned; incense may be placed on the burning charcoal

Charge: Words spoken by a deity through a member of the coven

Circle: *Consecrating,* done with saltwater and burning incense
Drawing, done with the sword
Sweeping, done with the besom or broomstick, moving sunwise

Cords of initiation: Three yard-long lengths of colored cord with ends bound but not knotted

Deosil: Sunwise

Divination: Reading tarot cards, runes, or other methods of telling fortunes

Esbat: Coven meeting on a nonfestival day

Evocation: Calling gods/goddesses into the circle

Great Rite, The: Making love, either symbolic or actual

Invocation: Calling gods/goddesses into a person

Libation: Offering thanks to the gods by pouring drink and scattering crumbs in the yard or onto the growing earth

Magical weapons: Also called "Tools," comprising: athame, white-handled knife, cords of initiation, sword, pentacle, censer, and (optional) scourge

Pentacle: Decorated board used for holding objects for consecration

Sabat: Coven meeting on a festival day

Scourge: Cat-o'-nine-tails used mainly by priestesses to discipline priests. Many covens do not see the need for one.

Scrying: Using a black mirror, crystal ball, tea leaves, or other objects to see the future

Sky-clad: Naked

White-handled knife: Ritual knife for writing on candles, cutting cord, etc. It is never taken out of the circle.

Widdershins: Countersunwise

Useful Addresses

Eye of the Cat, 3314E. Broadway, Long Beach, CA 90803.

Raven, 17 Melton Fields, Brickyard Lane, North Ferriby, East Yorkshire HU14 3HE, England.

Index